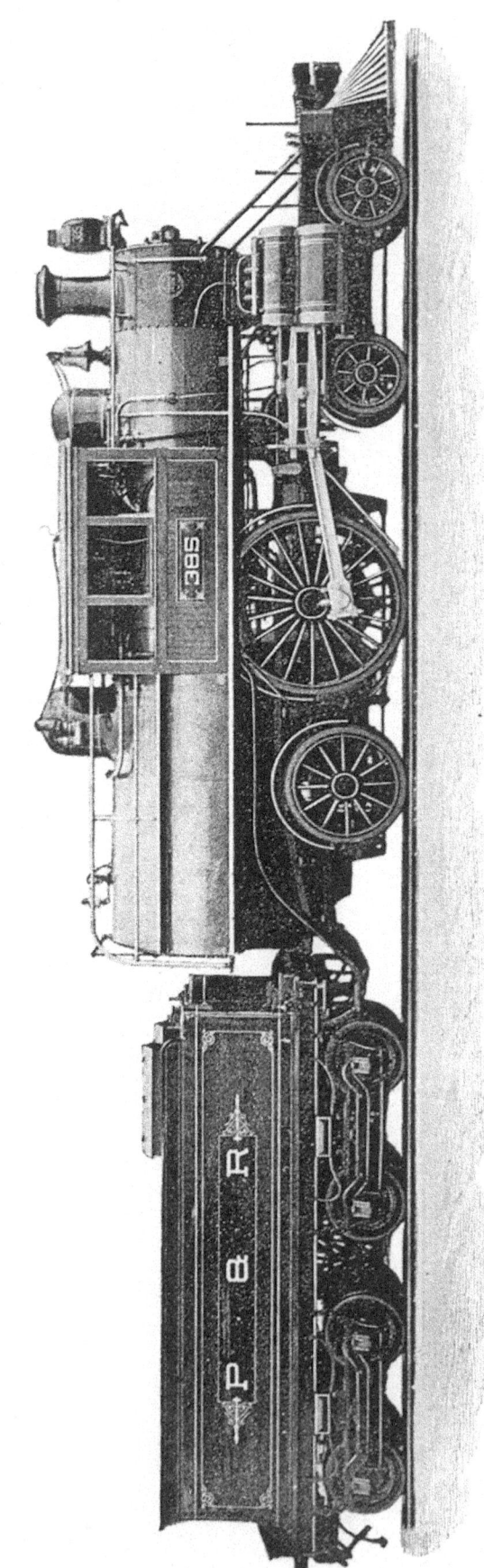

EXPRESS LOCOMOTIVE, WITH SINGLE PAIR OF DRIVING WHEELS, PHILADELPHIA & READING RAILROAD.

Description,

Method of Operation and Maintenance

of the

VAUCLAIN SYSTEM

of

COMPOUND LOCOMOTIVES.

BALDWIN LOCOMOTIVE WORKS,

BURNHAM, WILLIAMS & CO.,

PHILADELPHIA, PA.

©2007-2010 Periscope Film LLC
All Rights Reserved
ISBN #978-1-935700-15-9
www.PeriscopeFilm.com

BALDWIN LOCOMOTIVE WORKS,

BURNHAM, WILLIAMS & CO.,

PHILADELPHIA, PA.

Description,

Method of Operation and Maintenance

of the

VAUCLAIN SYSTEM

of

COMPOUND LOCOMOTIVES.

PATENTS.

Compound Locomotive Engine	No. 406,011, June 25, 1889.
Valve for Compound Engines	No. 406,012, June 25, 1889.
Combined Starting and Blow-off Valve	No. 471,836, March 29, 1892.
Starting Valve	No. 499,066, June 6, 1893.
Combined Starting and Drip Valve	No. 515,725, Feb. 27, 1894.
Relief Valves for Locomotives	No. 657,472, Sept. 4, 1900.
Valves for Compound Engines	No. 660,474, Oct. 23, 1900.

1900.

ATLANTIC TYPE LOCOMOTIVE, CHICAGO, BURLINGTON & QUINCY RAILROAD.
TAKEN WHILE RUNNING AT HIGH SPEED, SAID TO BE 75 MILES PER HOUR.

ATLANTIC TYPE LOCOMOTIVE, BALTIMORE & OHIO RAILROAD.

The "Vauclain" System

OF

COMPOUND LOCOMOTIVES.

DESCRIPTION.

In designing the "Vauclain" system of compound locomotives, the aim has been:

1. To produce a compound locomotive of the greatest efficiency, with the utmost simplicity of parts and the least possible deviation from existing practice. To realize the maximum economy of fuel and water.

2. To develop the same amount of power on each side of the locomotive, and avoid the racking of machinery resulting from unequal distribution of power.

3. To insure at least as great efficiency in every respect as in a single-expansion locomotive of similar weight and type.

4. To insure the least possible difference in cost of repairs.

5. To insure the least possible departure from the method of handling single-expansion locomotives; to apply equally to passenger or freight locomotives for all gauges of track, and to withstand the rough usage incidental to ordinary railroad service.

CONSOLIDATION LOCOMOTIVE, LEHIGH VALLEY RAILROAD. WEIGHT OF ENGINE IN WORKING ORDER, 230,000 POUNDS.

NARROW-GAUGE FREIGHT LOCOMOTIVE BAHIA EXTENSION.

The principal features of construction are as follows:

CYLINDERS.

The cylinders consist of one high-pressure and one low-pressure for each side, the ratio of the volumes being as nearly **three** to one as the employment of convenient measurements will allow. They are cast in one piece with the valve-chamber and saddle, the cylinders being in the same vertical plane, and as close together as they can be with adequate walls between them.

Where the front rails of the frames are single bars, the high-pressure cylinder is usually put on top, as shown in Fig. 1, but when the front rails of frames are double, the low-pressure cylinder is usually on top, as shown in Fig. 2.

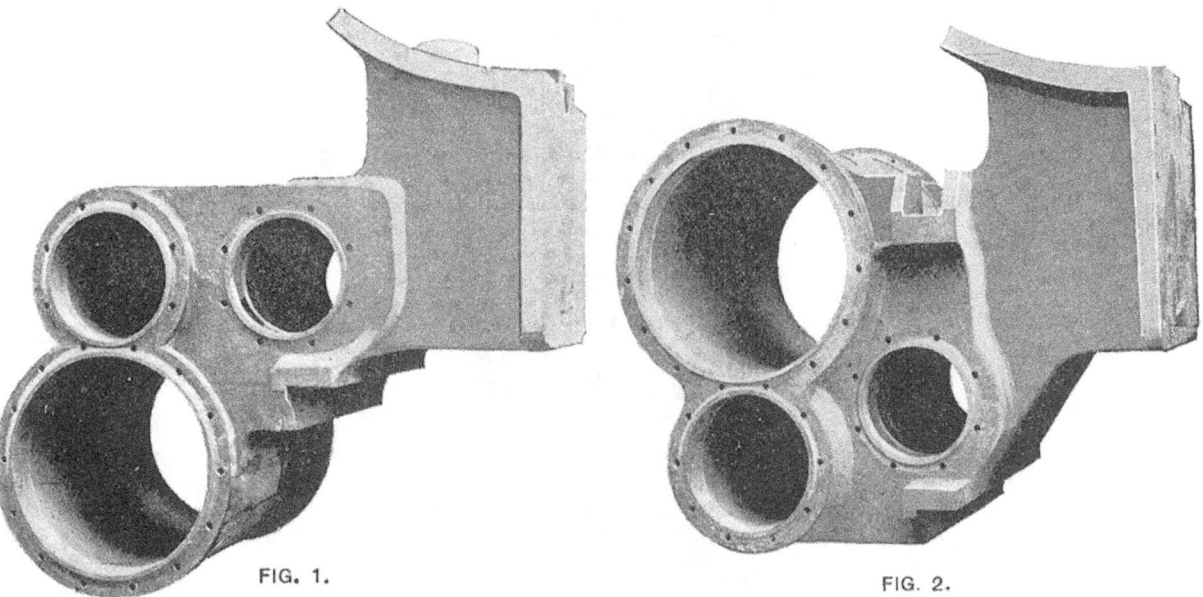

FIG. 1. FIG. 2.

TEN-WHEEL PASSENGER LOCOMOTIVE, CHICAGO, ROCK ISLAND & PACIFIC RAILWAY.

The former (Fig. 1) is used in "eight-wheel" or American type passenger locomotives, and in "ten-wheeled" locomotives, while the latter (Fig. 2) is used in Mogul, Consolidation and Decapod locomotives; for the various other classes of locomotives the most suitable arrangement is determined by the style of frames.

Fig. 3 shows the arrangement of the cylinders in relation to the valve.

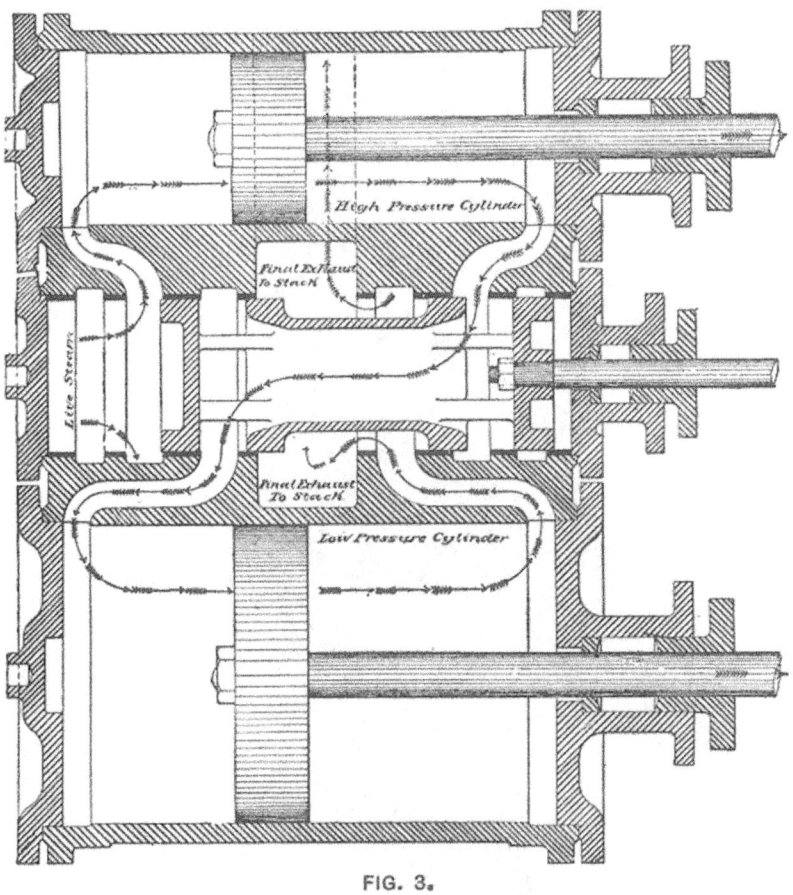

FIG. 3.

The valve employed to distribute the steam to the cylinders is of the piston type, working in a cylindrical steam-chest located in the saddle of the cylinder casting between the cylinders and the smoke-box, and as close to the cylinders as convenience will permit.

As the steam-chest must have the necessary steam passages cast in it and dressed accurately to the required sizes, the main passages in the cylinder casting leading thereto are cast wider than the finished ports. The steam-chest is bored out enough

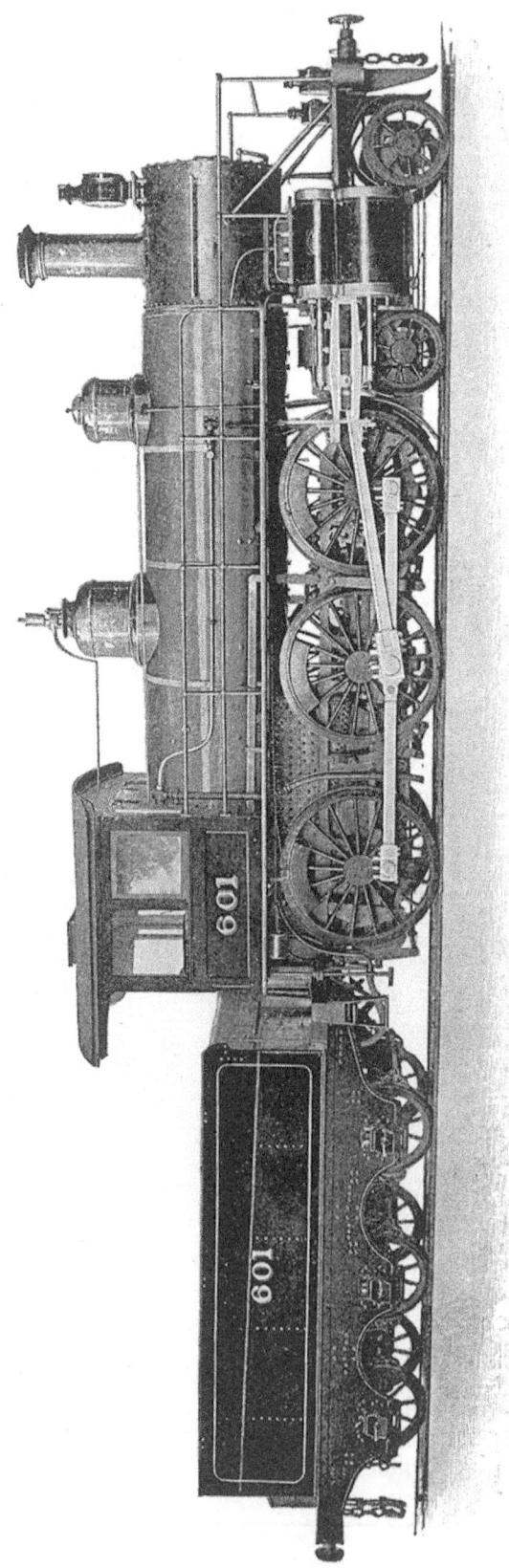

TEN-WHEEL PASSENGER LOCOMOTIVE SOUTHEASTERN RAILROAD OF RUSSIA.

larger than the diameter of the valve to permit the use of a hard cast iron bushing (Fig. 4). This bushing is forced into the steam-chest under such pressure as to prevent the escape of

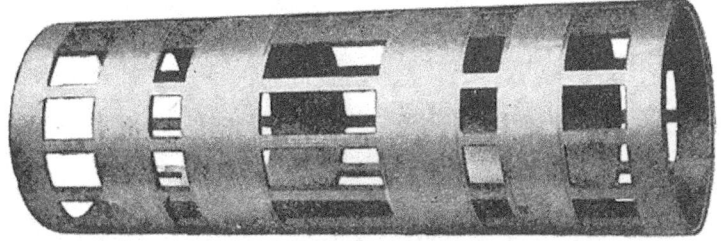

FIG. 4.

steam from one steam passage to another except by the action of the valve. Thus an opportunity is given to machine accurately all the various ports, so that the admission of steam is uniform under all conditions of service.

The valve, which is of the piston type,—double and hollow,—as shown by Fig. 5, controls the steam admission and exhaust of both cylinders. The exhaust steam from the high-pressure cylinder becomes the supply steam for the low-pressure cylinder.

FIG. 5.

As the supply steam for the high-pressure cylinder enters the steam-chest at both ends, the valve is in perfect balance, except the slight variation caused by the area of the valve-stem at the back end. This variation is an advantage in case the valve or its connection to the valve-rod should be broken, as it holds them together. Cases are reported where compound locomotives of this system have hauled passenger trains long distances with broken valve-stems and broken valves, the parts being kept in their proper relation while running by the compression due to the variation mentioned. To avoid the possibility of breaking, it

MOGUL FREIGHT LOCOMOTIVE, CHICAGO & ALTON RAILWAY.

is the present practice to pass the valve-stem through the valve and secure it by a nut on the front end.

Cast iron packing rings are fitted to the valve and constitute the edges of the valve. They are prevented from entering the steam-ports when the valve is in motion by the narrow bridge across the steam-ports of the bushing, as shown in Fig. 4. The operation of the valve is clearly shown by Fig. 3, the direction of the steam being indicated by arrows.

When the low-pressure cylinder is on top, as shown by Fig. 2, the double front rail prevents the use of the ordinary rock-shaft and box, and the valve motion is then what is called "direct acting," changing the location of the eccentrics on the axle in relation to the crank-pin. When the low-pressure cylinder is underneath, the rock-shaft is employed, and the eccentrics are placed in the usual position, the valve motion is termed "indirect acting." Fig. 6 shows the

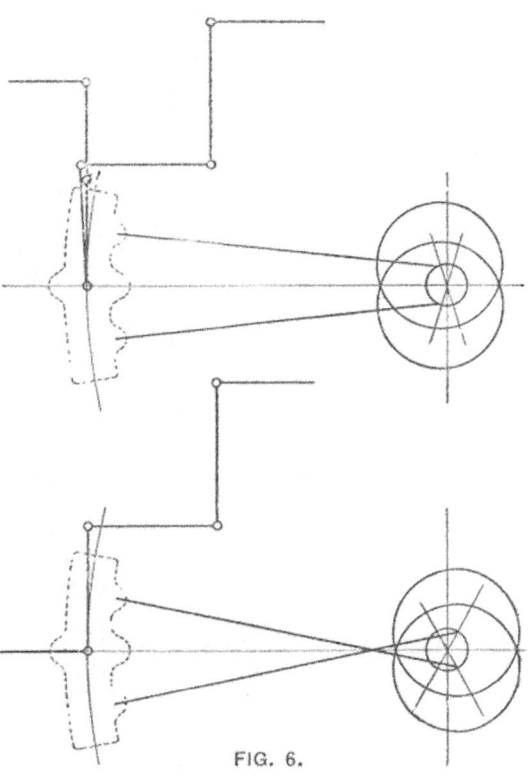

FIG. 6.

relation of the eccentrics with and without the rocker-shaft. Great care should be taken by mechanics, when setting the valves on these locomotives, to observe this difference and not get the eccentrics improperly located on the axle. If the crank-pin is placed on the forward centre, the eccentric-rods will not be crossed when the rocker-arm or indirect motion is used, but will be crossed when no rocker-arm or direct motion is used. Serious complications have arisen from this being disregarded.

In setting the piston valves, only the high pressure ports are to be considered. Both heads of the steam chest are removed and with a tram, from some point on the body of the cylinder to the valve stem, the line and line positions of the valve in both

TEN-WHEEL PASSENGER LOCOMOTIVE, CHICAGO, MILWAUKEE & ST. PAUL RAILWAY.

front and back motion, are laid off and indicated by a prick punch mark on the valve stem. Using the same tram, the position of the valve at different parts of the stroke can be ascertained, and the opening of the ports noted by the distance from the point of the tram to the prick punch mark. The relation of the low pressure ports to the valve must be ascertained by measurement, the same as the exhaust ports in ordinary slide valves.

Various methods have been employed to transfer the motion from the links to the valve-rod. That which has proved most satisfactory is to attach the ends of the link and valve-rods to the arms of an intermediate oscillating shaft. This arrangement allows for the free vertical movement of the end of the rod attached to the link, and gives a parallel movement to the valve-rod. It also makes it convenient to obtain any required lateral variation in the line of the two rods. These parts are thoroughly case-hardened,

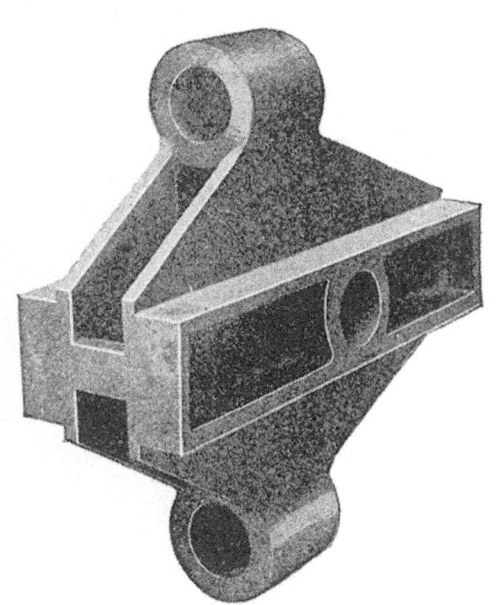

FIG. 7.

and with reasonable care should wear indefinitely. It is preferable, however, to use a rock-shaft when possible, as there is then less departure from ordinary locomotive practice.

The cross-head is shown by Fig. 7. It is made of open-hearth cast steel and is machined accurately to size. The bearings for the guide-bars are covered with a thin coating of block tin, about one-sixteenth inch thick, which wears well and prevents heating. The holes for the piston-rods are bored so that the

FIG. 8.

CONSOLIDATION LOCOMOTIVE, BALTIMORE & OHIO SOUTHWESTERN RAILWAY.

VAUCLAIN COMPOUND.

17

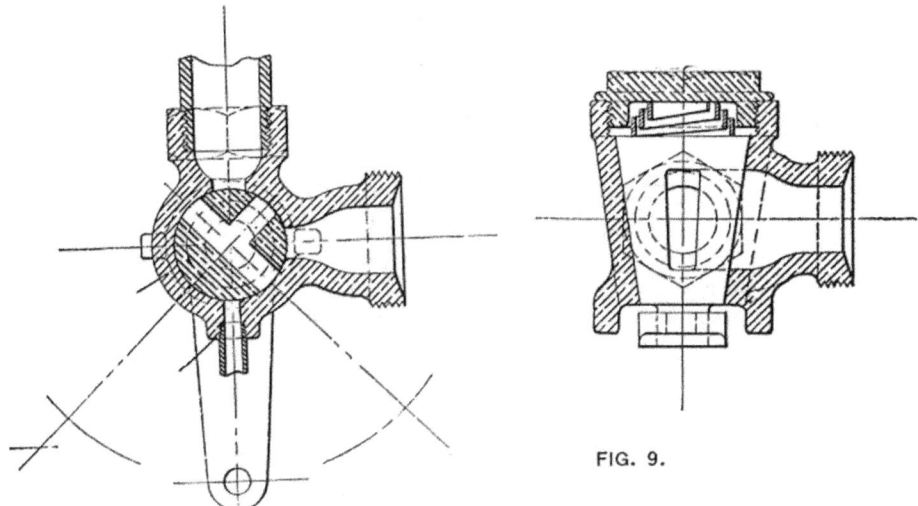

FIG. 9.

piston-rods will be perfectly parallel, and are tapered to insure a perfect fit.

The piston shown by Fig. 8 is made with either cast iron or cast steel heads, and is as light as possible. The rods, which are of triple-refined iron, are ground perfectly true to insure good service in connection with metallic packing for the stuffing boxes. The diameter of both piston-rods is the same, both having equal work to perform. They are made large enough to resist strains due to any unequal pressure that may come upon them in starting the locomotive from a state of rest. The cross-head end has a shoulder which prevents the piston-rod being forced into the cross-head, and at the same time permits the cross-head end and the body of the piston-rod to be of one diameter, thus permitting vibratory strains to act throughout the entire length of the rod instead of concentrating them at the shoulder next to the cross-head. The piston-rods are secured to the cross-head by large nuts, and these in turn are prevented from coming loose by taper keys driven tightly against them.

It is obvious that in starting these locomotives with full trains from a state of rest, it is necessary to admit steam to the low-pressure cylinder as well as to the high-pressure cylinder, which is accomplished by the use of a starting valve (Fig. 9). This is merely a pass-by valve which is opened to admit steam to pass from one end of the high-pressure cylinder to the other end and thence through the exhaust to the low-pressure cylinder. This is more clearly shown at E in Figs 11 and 12. The same cock acts as a

CONSOLIDATION LOCOMOTIVE, BAVARIAN STATE RAILWAYS.

cylinder cock for the high-pressure cylinder and is operated by the same lever that operates the ordinary cylinder cocks, thus making a simple and efficient device, and one that need not become disarranged. This valve should be kept shut as much as possible, as its indiscriminate use reduces the economy and makes the locomotive "logy."

As is usual in all engines, air valves are placed in the main steam passage of the high-pressure cylinder. Additional air valves, marked C and C^1 in Fig. 11, are placed in the steam passages of the low-pressure cylinders to supply them with sufficient air to prevent the formation of a vacuum, which would draw cinders into the steam-chest and cylinders.

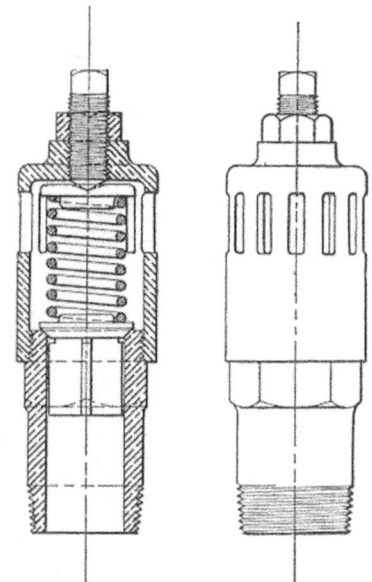

FIG. 10.

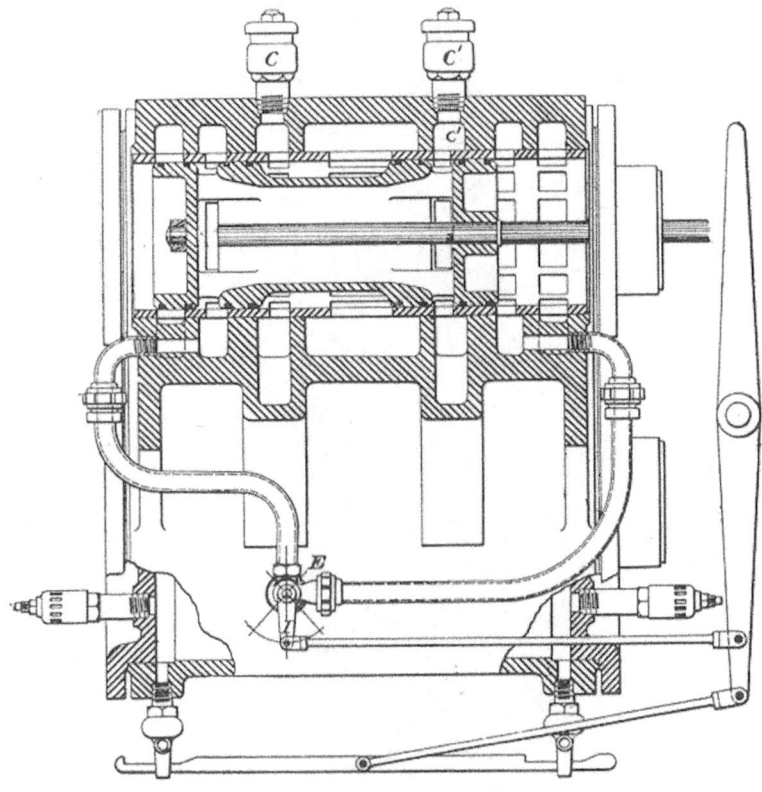

FIG. 11.

CONSOLIDATION LOCOMOTIVE, LEHIGH VALLEY RAILWAY, WEIGHT OF ENGINE IN WORKING ORDER, 200,000 POUNDS.

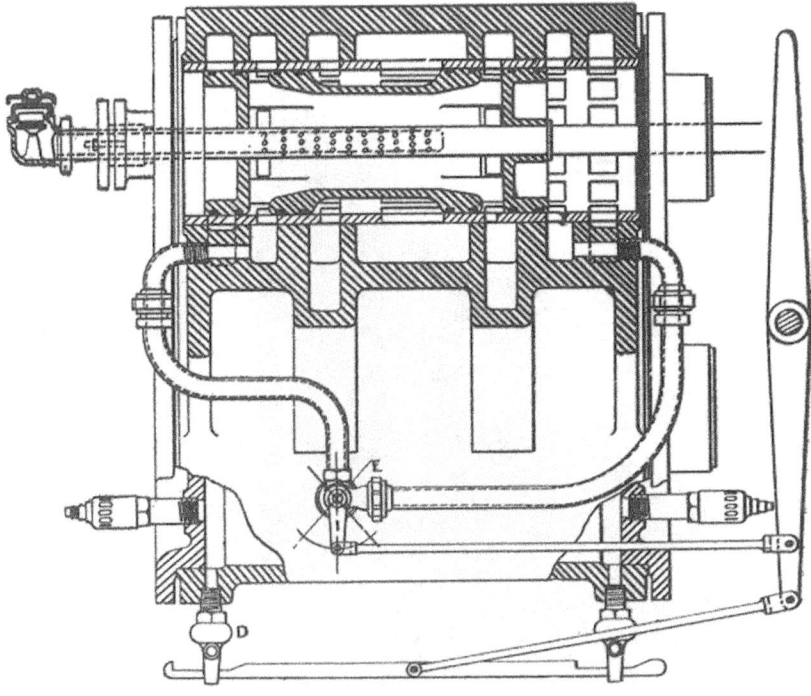

FIG. 12.

The hollow valve stem shown in Fig. 12 accomplishes the same result but with a more direct action and is preferable for fast service. The check valve at the end of the hollow stem outside the steam chest is closed by the pressure of the steam, but stands open when the pressure is relieved and air is allowed to pass into the valve through the perforation in the hollow stem. A vacuum is thus prevented from forming in the valve or low pressure passages. This arrangement will also prevent the accidental starting of the locomotive occasioned by a leaky throttle. The steam as it slowly escapes will pass through the hollow stem to the open air without creating pressure in the cylinders.

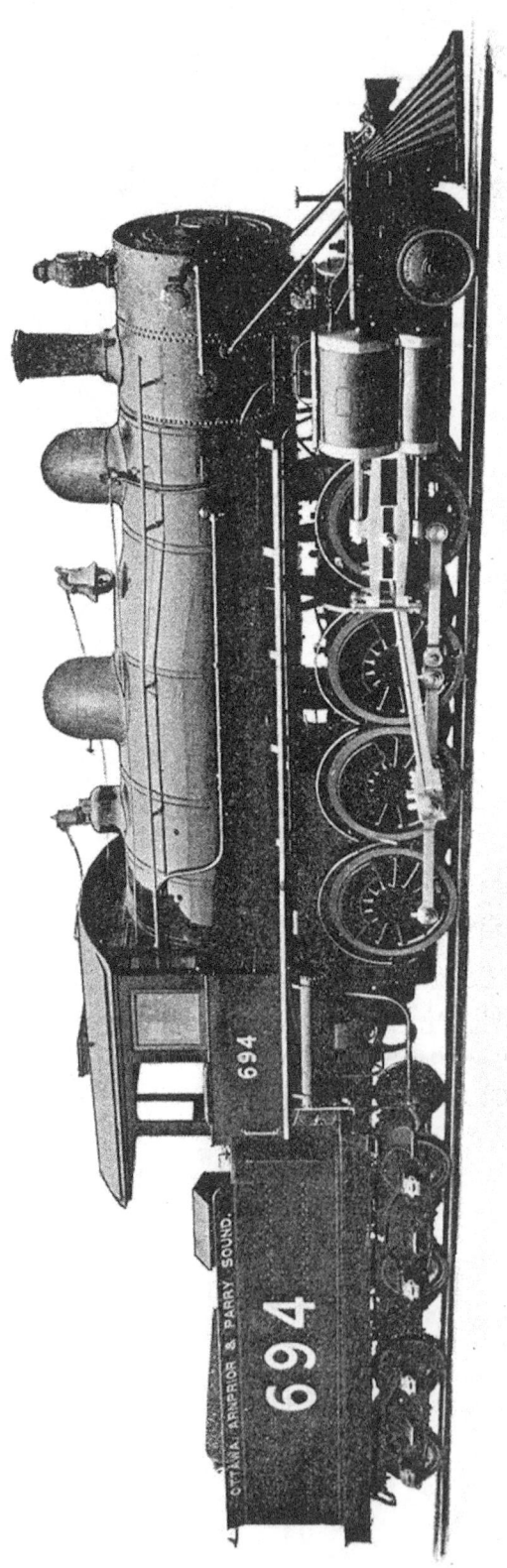

CONSOLIDATION LOCOMOTIVE, OTTAWA, ARNPRIOR & PARRY SOUND RAILROAD.

Water relief valves (Fig. 10) are applied to the low-pressure cylinders, and attached to the front and back cylinder heads, to prevent the rupture of the cylinder in case a careless engineer

SIX-COUPLED DOUBLE-ENDER LOCOMOTIVE, GOVERNMENT OF VICTORIA.

should permit the cylinders to be charged with water, or to relieve excessive pressure of any kind.

In all other respects the locomotive is the same as the ordinary single-expansion locomotive.

OPERATION.

It is not surprising, in view of their differences of opinion respecting single-expansion locomotives, that there has been much controversy among engineers and firemen in regard to the

SIX-COUPLED DOUBLE-ENDER LOCOMOTIVE, RAMAL FERREO CAMPINEIRO.

TEN-WHEEL LOCOMOTIVE, IOWA CENTRAL RAILWAY

operation of compound locomotives of this system. The first thing the engineer must learn is to use the reverse lever for what it is intended, that is, he must not hesitate to move it forward when ascending a grade if the locomotive shows signs of slowing up. The reverse quadrant is always so made that it is impossible to cut off steam in the high-pressure cylinder at less than half stroke, which avoids the damage that might ensue from excessive compression. It is perfectly practicable to operate the engine at any position of the reverse lever between half stroke and full stroke, without serious injury to the fire. When starting the

COMPRESSED AIR LOCOMOTIVE, PHILADELPHIA & READING COAL & IRON CO.

locomotive from a state of rest, the engineer should always open the cylinder cocks to relieve the cylinders of condensation, and as the starting valve is attached to the cylinder cocks, this movement also admits steam to the low-pressure cylinder and enables the locomotive to start quickly and freely. In case the locomotive is attached to a passenger train and standing in a crowded station, or in some position where it is undesirable to open the cylinder cocks, the engineer should move the cylinder cock lever in position to permit live steam to pass by into the low-pressure cylinder, thus enabling the locomotive to start quickly and uniformly, without any of the jerking motion so common in two-cylinder or cross-compound locomotives. After a few revolutions have been made and the cylinders are free from water caused by condensation or priming, the engineer should move

CONSOLIDATION LOCOMOTIVE, CHINESE EASTERN RAILWAY.

the cylinder cock lever into the central position, causing the engine to work compound entirely. This should be done before the reverse lever is disturbed from its full gear position. The reverse lever should never be "hooked up," thereby shortening the travel of the valve, until after the cylinder cock lever has been placed in the central position. It is often necessary to open the cylinder cocks when at full speed, to allow water to escape from the cylinders, especially when the engineer is what is commonly called a "high-water" man, and in such case no disadvantage is experienced and the reverse lever need not be disturbed. The starting device should not be used for any purpose other than the "starting" of the train. After the train is in motion it should not be used. Cases have been observed where the engineers use it all the time and have the reverse lever "hooked up" in the top notch (half stroke), in consequence of which the locomotive will slow down to a low speed whilst burning an excessive amount of coal. Such running must result in general dissatisfaction.

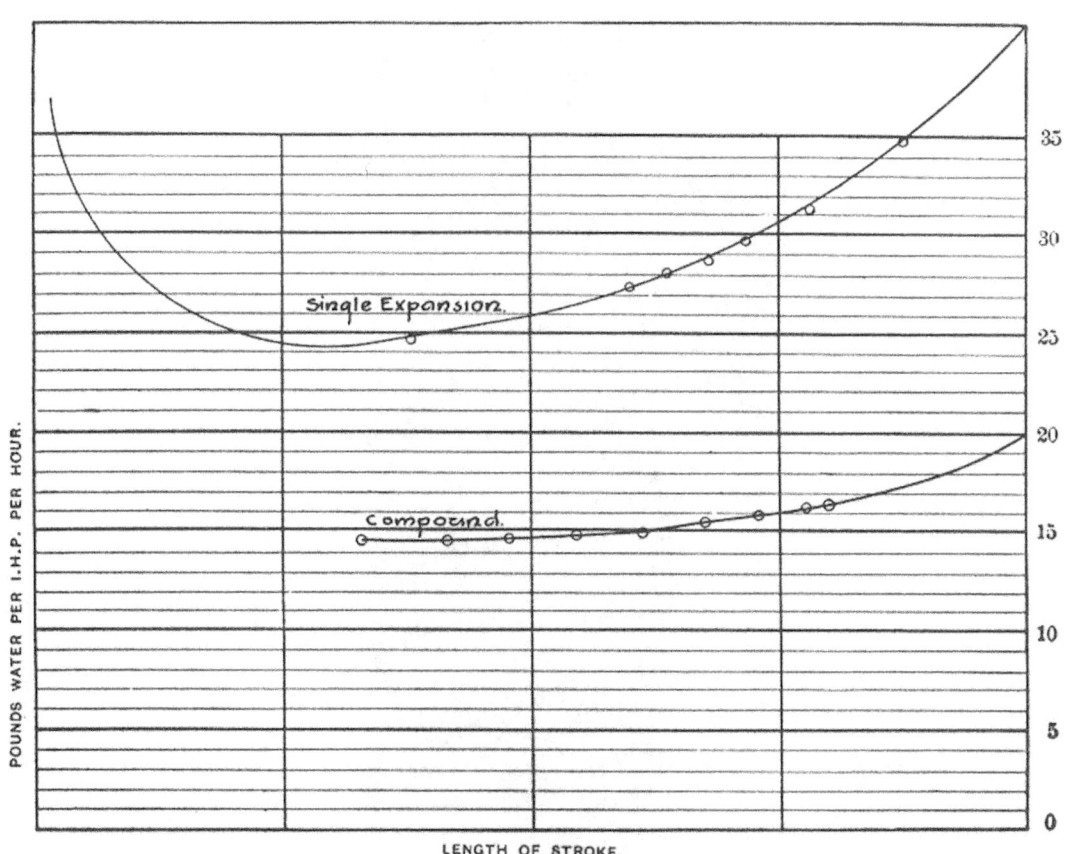

FIG. 13.

TEN-WHEEL LOCOMOTIVE, CHICAGO GREAT WESTERN RAILWAY.

The starting device is useful in emergencies, as, for instance, when stalling with a heavy train on a grade, if live steam is admitted to the low-pressure cylinder sufficient additional power is obtained to start the train and take it over the grade. This should be resorted to only in emergencies, and allowance should be made for the extra repairs caused by frequent cases of this kind.

On account of the very mild exhaust, the fireman should carry the fire as light as possible. A little practice will enable him to judge how to get along with the least amount of fuel.

The diagram (Fig. 13) page 27 shows the difference in the amount of water required to do the work at various points of cut-off in compound and single-expansion locomotives. The upper line shows the rate of water consumption per horse-power

DUPLEX LOCOMOTIVE, McCLOUD RIVER RAILROAD.

developed for several points of cut-off in single-expansion locomotives, whilst the lower line shows the same for compound locomotives. It will be observed that the most economical point of cut-off is about one-quarter stroke on the single-expansion locomotive, and about five-eighths stroke on the compound locomotive. It is also noticeable that the water-rate per horse-power varies very little on the compound locomotive when the reverse lever is moved towards full gear or longer cut-off, but in the single-expansion engine it increases rapidly, causing engineers to remark that they cannot "drop her a notch" on account of "getting away with the water." This does not occur with the compound locomotive when the reverse lever is moved forward towards full gear, and no engineer should open the pass-by valve, admitting

DECAPOD TYPE LOCOMOTIVE, MINNEAPOLIS, ST. PAUL & SAULT STE. MARIE RAILWAY

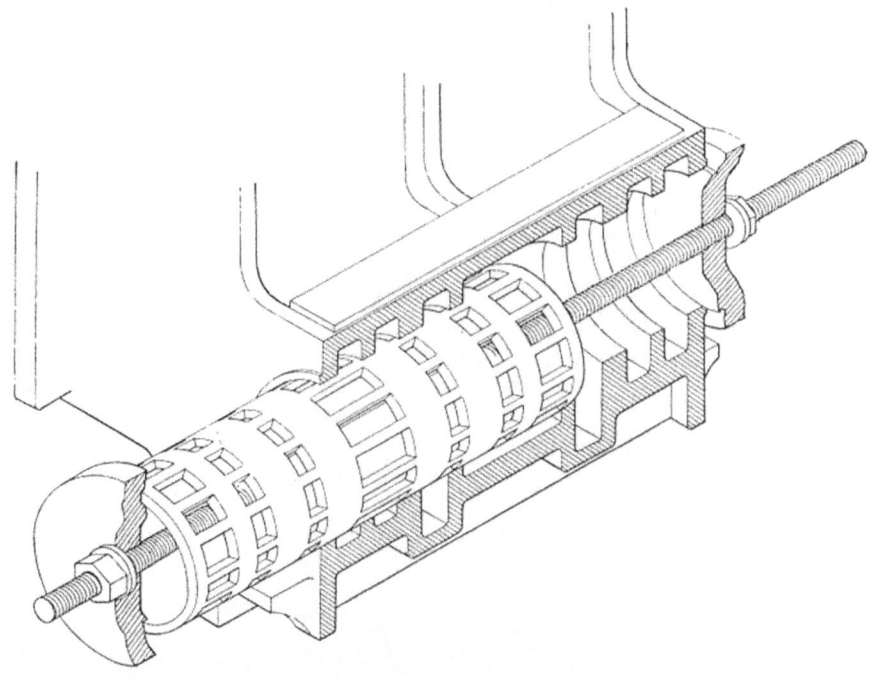

FIG. 14.

live steam to the low-pressure cylinder, until the last notch has been used on the quadrant and the engine is about to stall.

It is also desirable to move the reverse forward a notch before the locomotive slows down too much, as it is better to preserve the momentum of the train than to slow down and again have the trouble of accelerating. In this way both coal and water are wasted. If these instructions are observed the locomotive will work satisfactorily.

NARROW-GAUGE MOGUL LOCOMOTIVE, CENTRAL DOMINICAN RAILWAY.

CONSOLIDATION LOCOMOTIVE, IOWA CENTRAL RAILWAY.

REPAIRS.

On account of the great similarity to single-expansion locomotives, mechanics familiar with the latter have no difficulty in understanding these compound locomotives. There is no new element of repairs introduced,—no complicated starting or reducing valves, such as are common to other systems of compound locomotives.

The cross-heads, when badly worn, may, in a short time, be retinned by any coppersmith; in fact, an ordinary laborer can be taught this in a few days. The cross-head is heated warm enough to melt solder, and is then cleaned and wiped with solder, using dilute muriatic acid, such as tinsmiths use in soldering. Block tin is then poured against the surfaces so prepared, to which it

NARROW-GAUGE FOUR-COUPLED TANK LOCOMOTIVE, HAWAIIAN AGRICULTURAL CO., LTD.

adheres. A piece of iron placed alongside the cross-head can be used to regulate the thickness.

The cross-head is then put on a planer to true it up, care being used not to let the tool "dig in" and tear off the tin.

The pistons are treated the same as in ordinary single-expansion engines. The packing-rings in the low-pressure cylinder require renewal more frequently than those in high-pressure

TEN-WHEEL PASSENGER LOCOMOTIVE, BALTIMORE AND OHIO SOUTHWESTERN RAILWAY.

cylinders. It is also more difficult in compound cylinders to detect faulty packing-rings, and they are sometimes noticed only by the locomotive failing in steam and in not making time on the road.

The piston-valves should last a long time if properly lubricated, but when the bushing (Fig. 4) and valve (Fig. 5) are worn enough to require attention, the bushing should be bored out

SIX-COUPLED TANK LOCOMOTIVE, CHINESE EASTERN RAILWAY.

and new rings put in the valve; very often it is not necessary to bore the bushings, merely to put new packing-rings in the valve.

After the bushings (Fig. 4) have been bored several times, larger valves may be fitted to them so as to have as little play as possible. A very convenient type of boring bar for boring out the bushings has been designed, by which the work can be done without taking down the back head of the steam-chest. It is possible with this tool to bore out the bushings in less time than required to face a valve seat on a single-expansion locomotive.

When putting new bushings in the steam-chests, the device shown in Fig. 14 may be used, which gives the required power and is slow enough to permit the bushing to accommodate itself to the cylinder casting.

When extracting old bushings, it is best to split them with a narrow cape chisel—they are only fit for scrap when removed,

TEN-WHEEL PASSENGER LOCOMOTIVE, UNION PACIFIC RAILROAD.

and can be much more quickly removed this way than to attempt to draw them out with draw screws.

Enough attention should be given the starting valves to insure their moving in harmony with each other. Engineers sometimes strain the cylinder cock shaft, which causes one starting valve to open and the other to remain shut; this causes the exhaust to beat unevenly, and the engineer is apt to complain that the valves are out of square. Before altering the valve motion on these engines, make sure that the starting valves open and close simultaneously, and examine low-pressure pistons and piston valve for

RACK AND ADHESION LOCOMOTIVE, CIA MINERA DE PEÑOLES, MEXICO.

broken packing-rings. In one case an engineer ran his locomotive two days without any piston-head on one of the low-pressure pistons, and even then could not tell what was the matter, only that the locomotive sounded "lame" and did not make good time with the train. Men were put to work to locate the trouble, and found it, to the great surprise of the engineer.

ADDENDA.

It is not claimed for compound locomotives that a heavier train can be hauled at a given speed than with a single-expansion locomotive of similar weight and class. No locomotive can haul more than its adhesion will allow; but the compound will, at very slow speed on heavy grades, keep a train moving where a

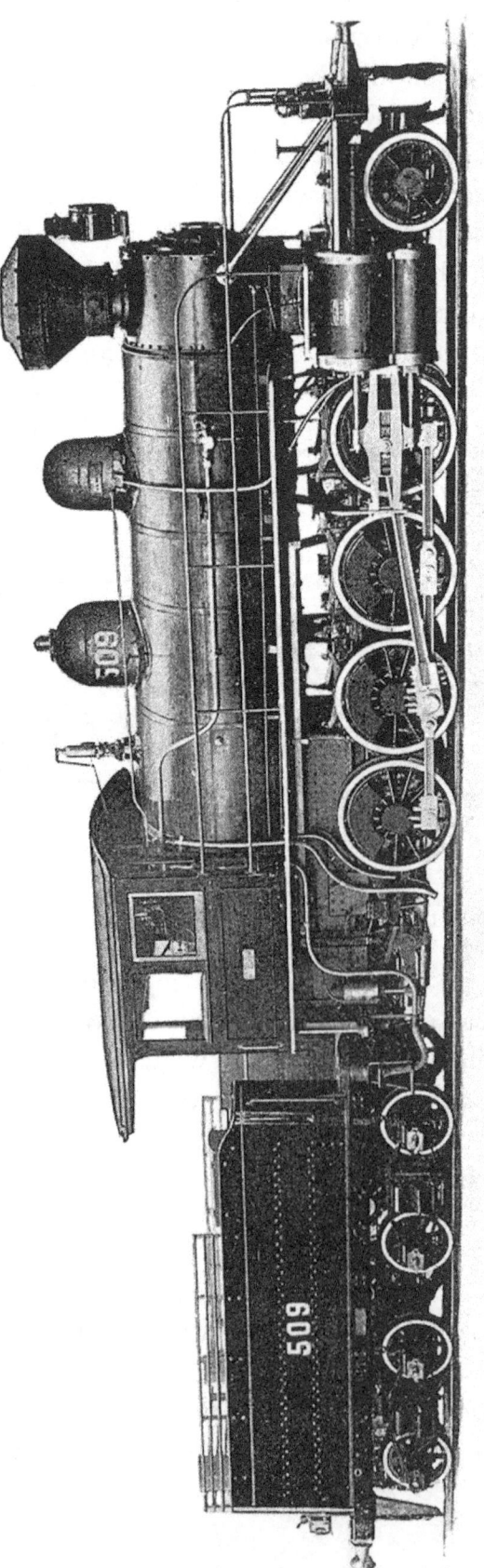

CONSOLIDATION LOCOMOTIVE, MOSCOW-WINDAU-RIBINSK RAILWAY OF RUSSIA.

single-expansion locomotive will slip and stall. This is due to the pressure on the crank-pins of the compound being more uniform throughout the stroke than is the case with the single-expansion locomotive.

The principal object in compounding locomotives is to effect fuel economy, and this economy is obtained,—

1. By the consumption of a smaller quantity of steam in the cylinders than is necessary for a single-expansion locomotive doing the same work.

2. The amount of water evaporated in doing the same work being less in the compound, a slower rate of combustion combined with a mild exhaust produces a higher efficiency from the coal burned.

In a stationary engine, which does not produce its own steam supply, it is of course proper to measure its efficiency solely by its economical consumption of steam. In an engine of this description the boilers are fired independently, and the draft is formed from causes entirely separate and beyond the control of the escape of steam from the cylinders; hence, any economy shown by the boilers must of necessity be separate and distinct from that which may be effected by the engine itself. In a locomotive, however, the amount of work depends entirely upon the weight on the driving-wheels, the cylinder dimensions being proportioned to this weight; and whether the locomotive is compound or single-expansion, no larger boiler can be provided, after allowing for the wheels, frames, and other mechanism, than this weight permits. Therefore, the heating surfaces and grate area are practically the same in both types, and the evaporative efficiency of both locomotives is determined by the action of the exhaust, which must be of sufficient intensity in both cases to generate the amount of steam necessary for utilizing, to the best advantage, the weight on the driving-wheels. This is is a feature that does not appear in a stationary engine, so that the compound locomotive cannot be judged by stationary standards, and the only true comparison to be made is between locomotives of similar construction and weight, equipped in one case with compound and in the other with single-expansion cylinders.

One of the legitimate advantages of the compound system is

that, owing to the better utilization of the steam, less demand is made upon the boiler, which enables sufficient steam-pressure to be maintained with the mild exhaust, due to the low tension of the steam when exhausted from the cylinders. This milder exhaust does not tear the fire, nor carry unconsumed fuel through the flues into the smoke-box and thence out of the smoke-stack, but is sufficient to maintain the necessary rate of combustion in

NARROW-GAUGE FOUR-COUPLED DOUBLE-ENDER ENCLOSED LOCOMOTIVE,
SAN JOSÉ & ALUM ROCK RAILWAY.

the fire-box with a decreased velocity of the products of combustion through the flues.

The heating surfaces of a boiler absorb heat units from the fire and deliver them to the water at a certain rate. If the rate at which the products of combustion are carried away exceeds the capacity of the heating surfaces to absorb and deliver the heat to the water in the boiler, there is a continual waste that can be overcome only by reducing the velocity of the products of combustion passing through the tubes. This is effected by the compound principle. It gives, therefore, not only the economy due to a smaller consumption of water for the same work, but the additional economy due to slower combustion. It is obvious that these two sources of economy are interdependent.

The improved action of the boiler can be obtained only by the use of the compound principle, while the use of the compound principle enables the locomotive to develop its full efficiency under conditions which in a single-expansion locomotive would require a boiler of capacity so large as to be out of the question under the circumstances usually governing locomotive construction. It is therefore evident that where both locomotives are exact duplicates in all their parts, excepting the cylinders, the improved action of the boiler is due entirely to the compound principle, and the percentage of economy should be based upon the total saving in fuel consumption, and not upon the water consumption, as in stationary practice.

For the benefit of those who may test these locomotives, the following method is presented of determining the water rate per horse-power from an indicator diagram:

S = Stroke in inches.
C = Per cent. of stroke completed at cut-off.
P = Pressure of steam at cut-off, taken from zero.
Wp = Weight per cubic foot of steam at P pressure.
H = Per cent. of stroke uncompleted at compression.
Q = Pressure of steam at compression, taken from zero.
Wq = Weight per cubic foot of steam at Q Pressure.
E = Per cent. of clearance in H.-P. cylinders.
A = Area of H.-P. cylinders.
P = M.E.P. of H.-P. cylinders.
a = Area of L.-P. cylinders.
K = M.E.P. of L.-P. cylinders.
N = Number of revolutions per minute.
r = Ratio $\frac{a}{A}$; hence, $a = A \times r$.

All calculations are made on the basis of the high-pressure cylinder doing the work of both cylinders.

The volume of the piston displacement is $A S$, and the volume at cut-off is $A S C$, since C is the proportion of stroke completed at cut-off. The volume of N revolutions would be $A N S C$. As there are two strokes of the piston for each revolution, and there is an engine on each side of the locomotive, assuming that both engines are doing exactly the same work, there would be four strokes per revolution; hence $4 A N S C$ is the volume of piston displacement at cut-off for one revolution. Since the clearance-space is expressed in percentage of the piston displace-

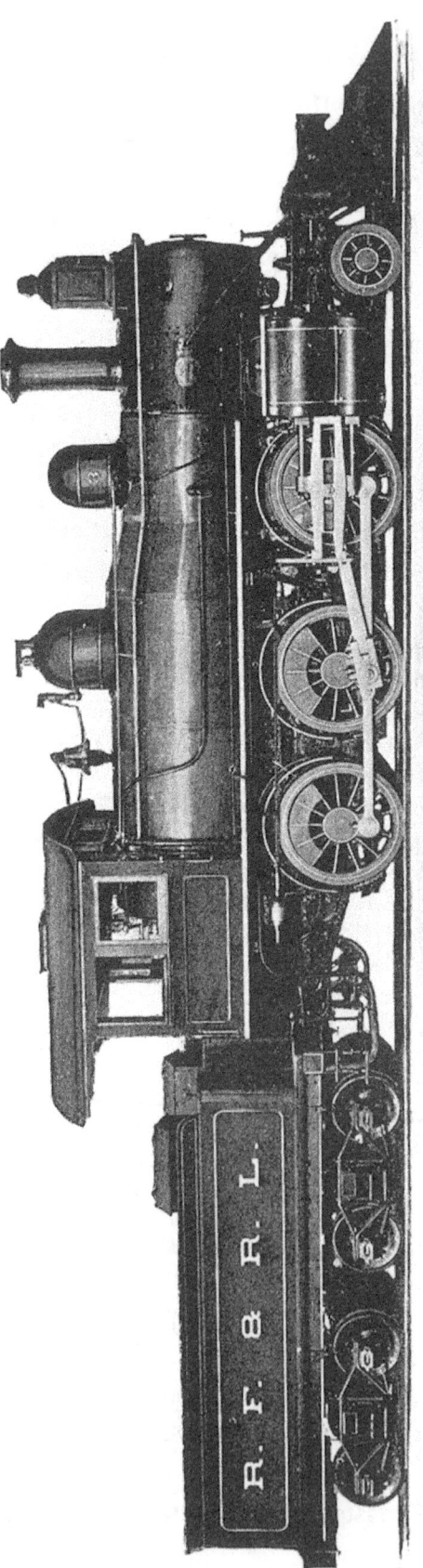

MOGUL FREIGHT LOCOMOTIVE, RUMFORD FALLS & RANGELEY LAKES RAILROAD.

ment of one stroke, and which space is filled at each stroke, the volume of the clearance-space for one revolution would be $4\,A\,N\,S\,E$. The sum of these two quantities divided by 1728 will give the volume in cubic feet. The indicator-card gives the pressure at cut-off, and a reference to the steam-table will give the weight of steam at that pressure; hence, the amount of steam used per revolution becomes $\left(\dfrac{4\,A\,N\,S\,C + 4\,A\,N\,S\,E}{1728}\right) Wp$. But there is a certain amount of steam saved at compression, and the volume at this point would be $\left(\dfrac{4\,A\,N\,S\,H + 4\,A\,N\,S\,E}{1728}\right) Wq$. The volume of the clearance space being again taken into consideration. Since this steam is saved by compression, it should be deducted from the amount used, and the formula becomes:

$$\left(\dfrac{4\,A\,N\,S\,C + 4\,A\,N\,S\,E}{1728}\right) Wp - \left(\dfrac{4\,A\,N\,S\,H + 4\,A\,N\,S\,E}{1728}\right) Wq;$$

or $\dfrac{4\,A\,N\,S}{1728}\Big((C+E)Wp - (H+E)Wq\Big)$. The H.-P. equals $\dfrac{4\,A\,N\,S(P + rK)}{12 \times 33{,}000}$. Then the water rate per minute would be

$$\dfrac{\dfrac{4\,A\,N\,S}{1728}\Big((C+E)Wp - (H+E)Wq\Big)}{\dfrac{4\,A\,N\,S(P + rK)}{12 \times 33{,}000}}, \text{ or } \dfrac{229.16}{P + rK}\Big((C+E)Wp - (H+E)Wq\Big);$$

and the rate per hour would be $\dfrac{60 \times 229.16}{P + rK}$, or $\dfrac{13750}{P + rK}\Big((C+E)Wp - (H+E)Wq\Big)$, which formula is to be used.

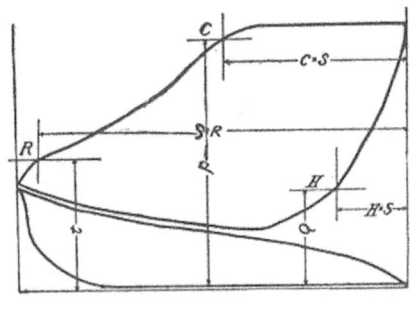

FIG. 15.

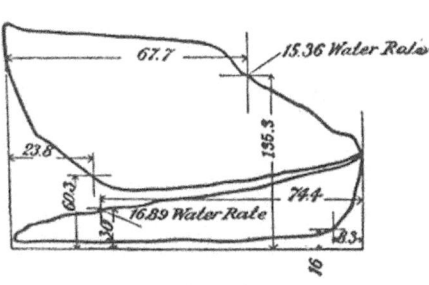

FIG. 16.

If it is desired to get the steam at release H.-P., substitute the value of the point R and pressure t, also $S \times R$, respectively, for C, p, and $C \times S$. See Figs. 15 and 16.

    M.E.P. H.-P. cylinder . . . . 87 pounds   Clearance 08
    M.E.P. L.-P. cylinder . . . 32 pounds   Ratio . . . . 2.87 to 1
    M.E.P. referred to H.-P. cylinder 178.84
    M.E.P. referred to L.-P. cylinder 62.31

$$178.84 = P + r\,K$$
$$62.31 = K + \frac{P}{r}$$

135.3
14.7
―――
150.0 = .3376 pound per cubic foot of steam at cut-off H.-P. cylinder.

60.3
14.7
―――
75.0 = .1756 pound per cubic foot of steam at compression H.-P. cylinder.

30.
14.7
―――
44.7 = .1079 pound per cubic foot of steam at point on L.-P. expansion line.

16.
14.7
―――
30.7 = .0758 pound per cubic foot of steam at compression L.-P. cylinder.

$$\frac{13750}{178.84} = 76.88 \qquad \frac{13750}{62.31} = 220.67$$

$(.677 + .08) \times .3376 = .2556 \qquad (.238 + .08) \times .1756 = .0558$

.2556
.0558
―――
.1998

.1998 × 76.88 = 15.36 pounds steam at cut-off H.-P. cylinder.

$(.744 + .08) \times .1079 = .0889 \qquad (.083 + .08) \times .0758 = .0124$

.0889
.0124
―――
.0765

.0765 × 220.67 = 16.89 pounds steam at point on expansion line L.-P. cylinder.

VAUCLAIN COMPOUND. 45

The following method of combining indicator diagrams, devised by Mr. George H. Barrus, is given also, and is generally accepted by all engineers as the correct method.

METHOD OF COMBINING CARDS.

(FURNISHED BY MR. GEORGE H. BARRUS.)

The method employed corresponds to that given in Rankine's book on the steam-engine, but is here given more in detail. This method will be clearly understood if it is remembered that every point in the expansion line of the L.-P. card of the combined diagram should correctly represent the pressure and volume of the steam at the corresponding point of the stroke of the low-pressure piston, the volume being measured from the clearance line of that cylinder. Referring to Fig. 17, the H.-P. diagram is an exact copy of the original except in point of scale. The L.-P. diagram at the bottom of Fig. 17 is also an exact

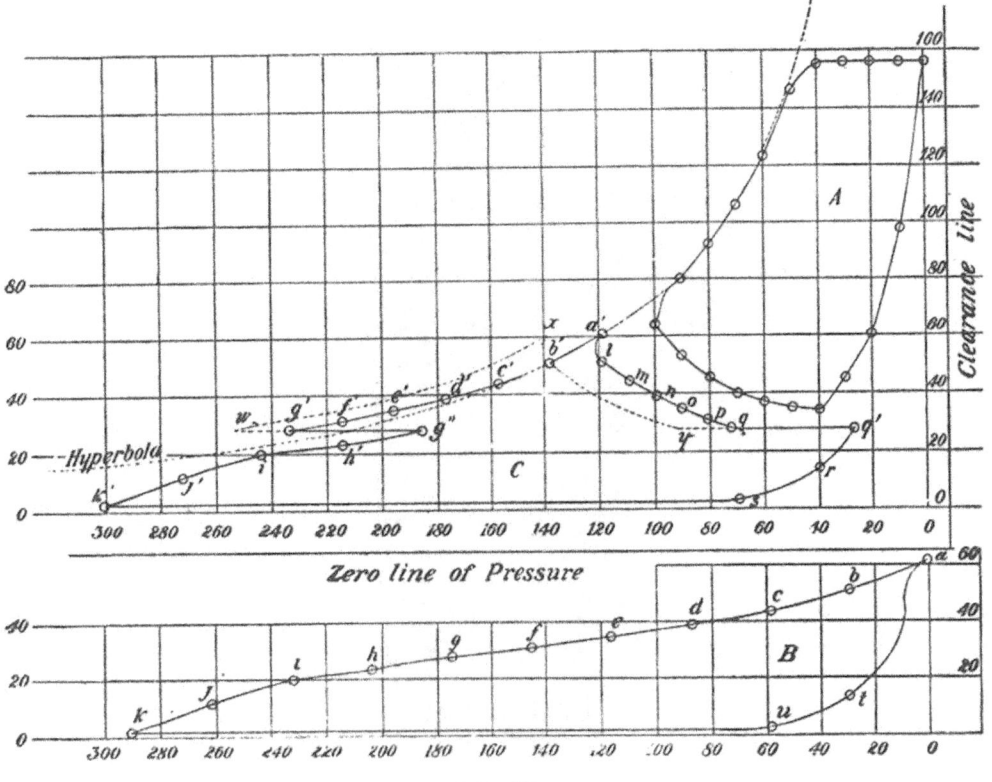

FIG 17

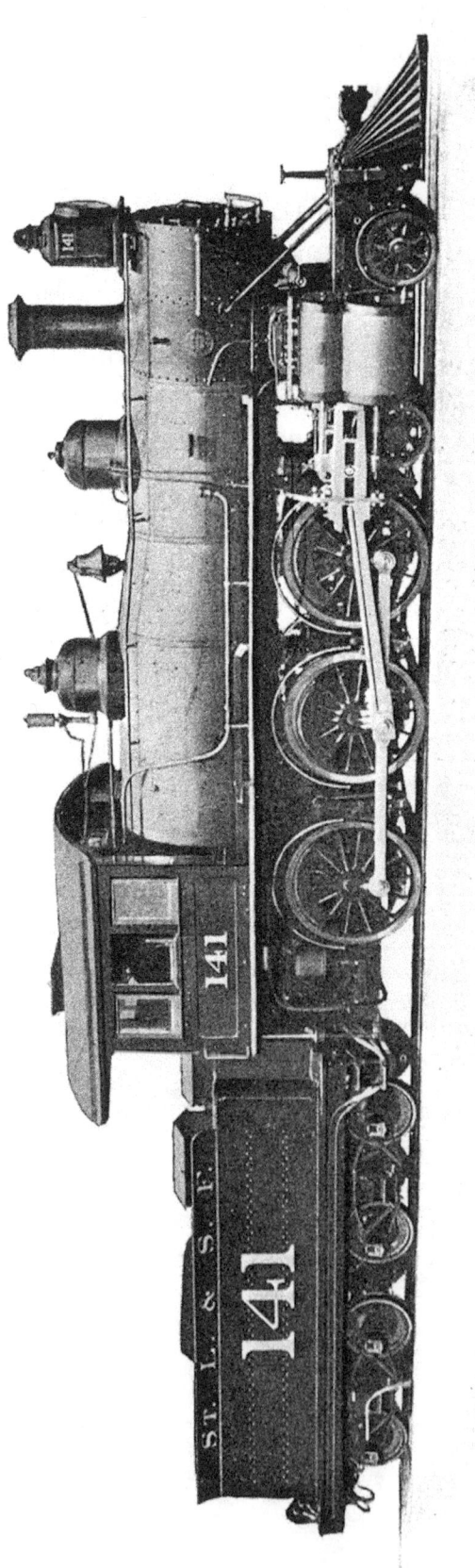

TEN-WHEEL LOCOMOTIVE, ST. LOUIS AND SAN FRANCISCO RAILWAY.

copy of the original on the same scale of pressure as the H.-P. diagram, though of different length; this last having the same ratio to the length of the H.-P. diagram as the area of the piston of the L.-P. cylinder has to the area of that of the high; in this case 2.9. The length of the H.-P. diagram on the scale of the chart is 100, as indicated, and of the L.-P. diagram 290.

To draw the L.-P. portion of the diagram, it may be divided into, say, ten equal parts, and the points of the division marked

RACK LOCOMOTIVE, S. ELLERO & VALLOMBROSA.

$a, b, c, d,$ and e. The various points on the combined L.-P. diagram are located horizontally, so as to mark the various volumes occupied by the steam at the respective points, as already noted. Below the point of cut-off, which is located at .6 of the stroke, or at the point 9, the combined diagram is an exact reproduction of the lower diagram. The points in this portion of the diagram showing volume, that is, the horizontal distances, represent the volumes of the L.-P. cylinders at those points, plus the clearance of the same. The clearance is 6.5 per cent. of the stroke of the L.-P. piston, or is 18.9 points of division on the scale of the chart. The distance, for example, of the point h from the clearance line on the combined diagram, will be .7 of $290+19$, or $203+19=222$, and likewise for the remaining points below the cut-off. The

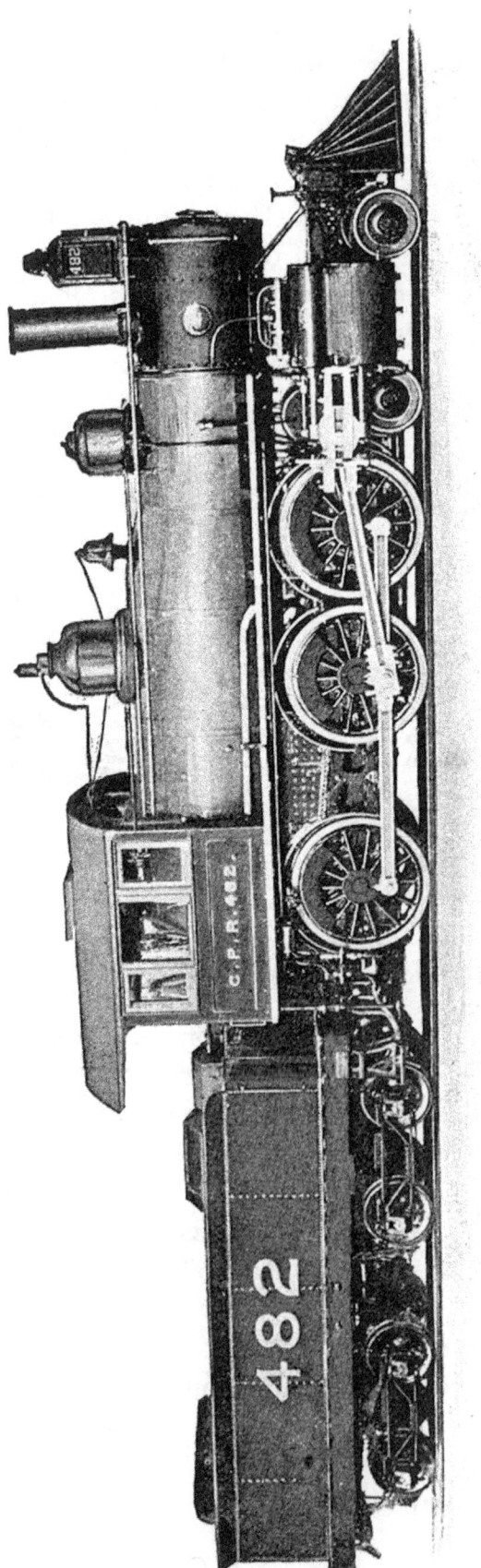

TEN-WHEEL LOCOMOTIVE, CANADIAN PACIFIC RAILWAY.

points in the expansion line of the L.-P. combined diagram, above the points of cut-off, lie farther to the left, for the reason that the volume of the steam expanding is not only the apparent volume of that contained in the L.-P .cylinder, but in addition, that of the steam being exhausted from the H.-P. cylinder (the valve being open between the two), and that contained in the clearance space of the same. Take, for instance, the point a', or the initial point of the diagram; the volume here is that of the H.-P. cylinder, the clearance of the H.-P. cylinder, and the clearance of the L.-P. cylinder. The point a' is therefore laid off at a distance of 19 divisions to the left of the end of the H.-P. diagram, or at the division marked 119 on the chart. At the point b' the volume of the steam has been increased, corresponding to 1-10 of the L.-P. cylinder, or 29 divisions, but at the same time it has been reduced correspondingly to 1-10 of the

FOUR-COUPLED SIX-WHEEL TANK LOCOMOTIVE STATE TRANSCAUCASIAN.

H.-P. cylinder, or to 10 divisions, so that the combined effect is to increase the volume 19 divisions to the left of the point a'. The remaining points from b' to g' are laid off successively at distances of 19 divisions. At g', where the valve closes and cuts off communications between the H.-P. and L.-P. cylinders, the volume contracts, and this feature is represented by the horizontal line $g'\ g''$. To obtain the remaining points of the

TEN-WHEEL LOCOMOTIVE, CLEVELAND, CINCINNATI, CHICAGO & ST. LOUIS RAILWAY.

combined diagram from a' to q', the various points are laid off, so that the horizontal distances from the expansion line shall be the same as those in the lower diagram. In this way the area of the combined diagram is exactly the same as that of the original diagram. The dotted line $x\ w\ y$ shows the position of the combined diagram, supposing the intermediate space within the valve were empty when the H.-P. cylinder exhausted, assuming that the volume of this space is 20 per cent. of the volume of the H.-P. cylinder. In reality this space is not empty, but is always filled with steam somewhat above the pressure at cut-off in L.-P. cylinder.

SUGGESTIONS FOR RUNNING A VAUCLAIN FOUR-CYLINDER COMPOUND LOCOMOTIVE.

In starting the locomotive with a train, place the reverse lever in full forward position, throw the cylinder-cock lever forward, which operation opens the starting-valve and allows live steam to pass to the low-pressure cylinder. The throttle is then opened, and as soon as possible when the cylinders are free of water and the train is under good headway, the cylinder cocks and starting-valve should be closed. As the economy of a compound locomotive depends largely on its greater range of expansion, the engineer should bear in mind that in order to get the best results he must use his reverse lever. After the starting-valve is closed and as the speed of the train increases, the reverse lever should be hooked back a few notches at a time until the full power of the locomotive is developed. If after moving the reverse lever to the last notch, which cuts off the steam at about half stroke in the high-pressure cylinder, it is found that the locomotive develops more power than is required, the throttle must be partially closed and the flow of steam to the cylinder reduced. On slightly descending grades the steam may be throttled very close, allowing just enough in the cylinders to keep the air-valves closed. If the descent is such as to prevent the use of steam, close the throttle and move the reverse lever

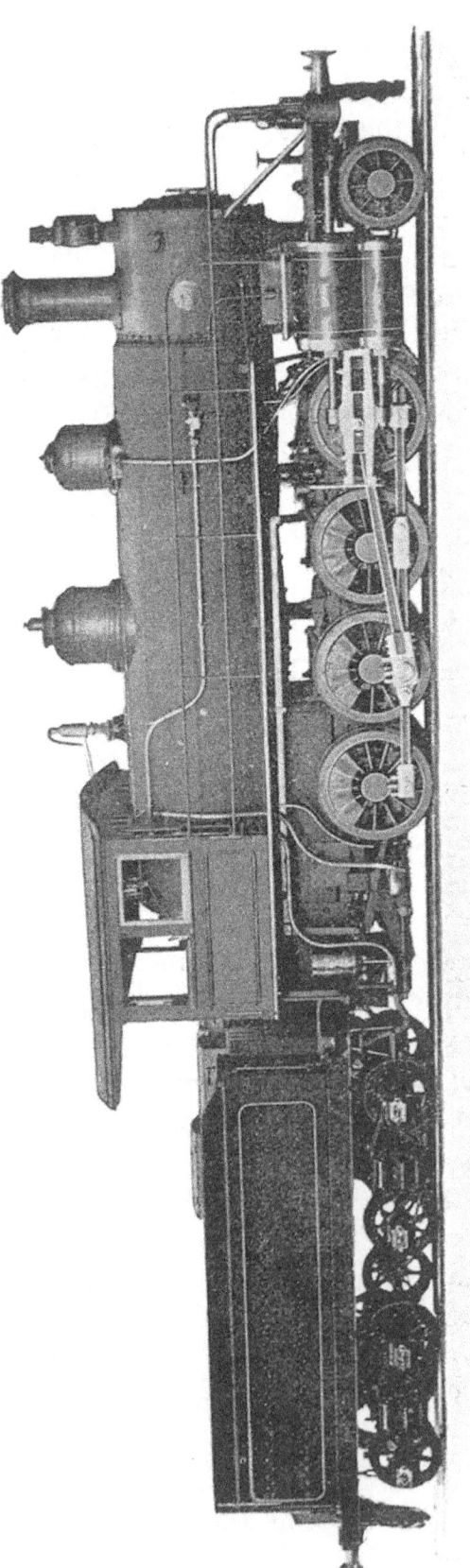

CONSOLIDATION LOCOMOTIVE, SOUTHEASTERN RAILWAY OF RUSSIA.

gradually to the forward notch and move the starting-valve lever to its full backward position. This allows the air to circulate either way through the starting-valve from one side of the piston to the other, relieves the vacuum, and prevents the oil from being

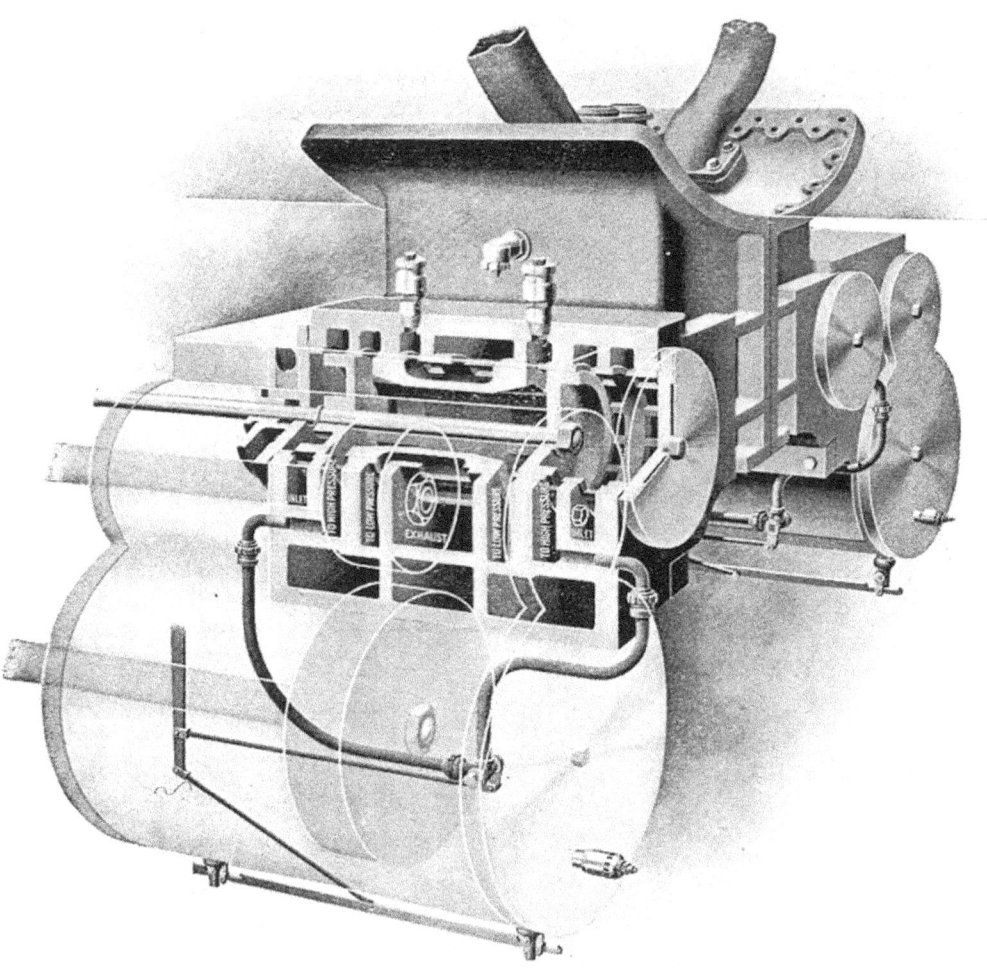

VIEW SHOWING GENERAL ARRANGEMENT OF CYLINDERS, WITH SECTION THROUGH STEAM CHEST VALVE AND PORTS.

blown out of the cylinder. On ascending grades with heavy loads as the speed decreases the reverse lever should be moved forward sufficiently to keep up the required speed. If, after the reverse lever is placed in the full forward notch, the speed still decreases and there is danger of stalling, the starting-valve may be used, admitting steam to the low-pressure cylinders. This should be done only in cases of emergency and the valve closed as soon as the difficulty is overcome.

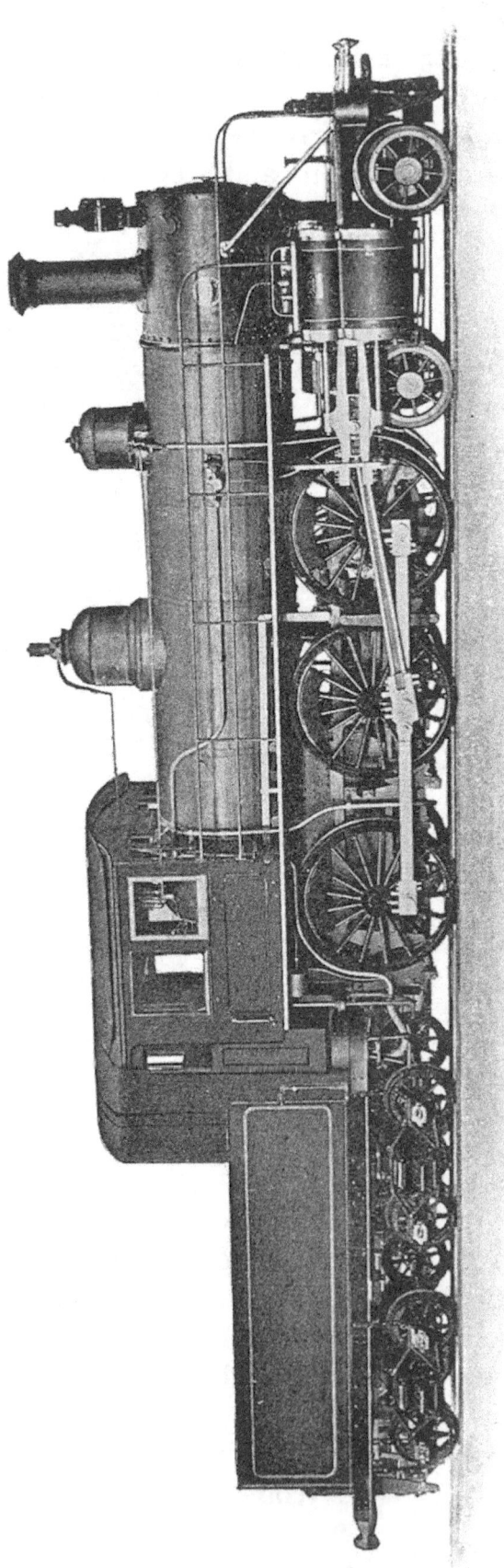

TEN-WHEEL LOCOMOTIVE, MOSCOW-KIEF-VORONEJE RAILWAY, RUSSIA.

VAUCLAIN COMPOUND.

The tractive power of Vauclain four-cylinder compound locomotives may be ascertained by the following formula:

$$\frac{C^2 \times S \times \tfrac{2}{3} P}{D} + \frac{c^2 \times S \times \tfrac{1}{4} P}{D} = T, \text{ in which}$$

$C=$Diameter of high-pressure cylinder in inches.
$c=$Diameter of low-pressure cylinder in inches.
$S=$Stroke of piston in inches.
$P=$Boiler pressure in pounds.
$D=$Diameter of driving wheels in inches.
$T=$Tractive power.

The first Vauclain compound locomotive was built in 1889; in the year 1890 three more were built, followed in 1891 by 82, in 1892 by 213, in 1893 by 160, in 1894 by 30, in 1895 by 51, in 1896 by 173, in 1897 by 86, in 1898 by 235, in 1899 by 241,

MOGUL FREIGHT LOCOMOTIVE, NORTHERN PACIFIC RAILROAD.

and in 1900 there have been built or orders have been received for 591. Those already shipped are distributed among the various railroad companies as follows:

Algoma Central	1
Altoona, Clearfield and Northern	1
Altoona and Phillipsburg Connecting	2
Arizona and South Eastern	1
Atlantic Coast Line	2
Bahia Extension, Brazil	11
Baltimore and Ohio	167

CONSOLIDATION LOCOMOTIVE, BALTIMORE & OHIO RAILROAD.

ATLANTIC TYPE LOCOMOTIVE, ERIE RAILROAD.

Baltimore and Ohio Southwestern	47
Barranquilla Railway	2
Bavarian State Railways	4
Brazilian Industrial Improvement Co.	3
Brooklyn Wharf and Warehouse Co.	2
Buffalo, Rochester and Pittsburg	6
Buenos Aires Western	2
Calumet and Hecla	1
Cambria Steel Co. (compressed air)	1
Canadian Pacific	34
Central Dominican	3
Central of Georgia	3
Central Railroad of Brazil	23
Central Railroad of New Jersey	14
Chicago and Alton	15
Chicago and Erie	2
Chicago and Grand Trunk	1
Chicago and Great Western	15
Chicago and Northwestern	3
Chicago and South Side	45
Chicago, Burlington and Quincy	5
Chicago, Milwaukee and St. Paul	115
Chicago, Rock Island and Pacific	22
Chilean State Railways	4
Chinese Eastern	148
Cia Minera de Peñoles, Mexico (rack)	4
Cincinnati, Hamilton and Dayton	1

Cincinnati, New Orleans and Texas Pacific.............. 12
Cleveland, Akron and Columbus 2
Cleveland, Cincinnati, Chicago and St. Louis............ 2
Columbia University................................. 1
Cornwall and Lebanon............................... 2
Consolidation Coal Co. (compressed air)............... 2
Delaware, Lackawanna and Western 1
Egyptian State Railways 1
Elgin, Joliet and Eastern 1
Engenho Central, Brazil 1
Erie 84

ATLANTIC TYPE LOCOMOTIVE, CANADA ATLANTIC RAILWAY.

F. C. del Norté 3
F. C. de Merida á Valladolid......................... 1
Fitchburg 7
French State Railways 5
Frick Coke Co. (compressed air)..................... 5
Great Northern 7
Government New South Wales, Australia.............. 2
Grand Trunk....................................... 10
Hamilton and Dundas 1
Hawaiian Agricultural Co............................ 1
Hidalgo Railroad, Mexico 1

Intercolonial Railway of Canada	20
Interoceanic of Mexico	2
Iowa Central	7
Jacksonville, Tampa and Key West	1
Kansas City Southern	10
Kentucky Union	1
Lehigh and Lackawanna	2

RACK LOCOMOTIVE, MANITOU AND PIKES PEAK RAILWAY.

Lehigh Coal and Navigation Co.	2
Lehigh Valley	89
Leopoldina Railway, Brazil	1
Long Island	15
Longdale Iron Co.	3
Los Angeles Terminal	1
McCloud River	1
Marietta and North Georgia	1
Mexican National	32
Mineral Range	1
Minneapolis, St. Paul and Sault Ste. Marie	2
Missouri, Kansas and Texas	17
Mogyana Railroad, Brazil	1
Moscow Kazan	2

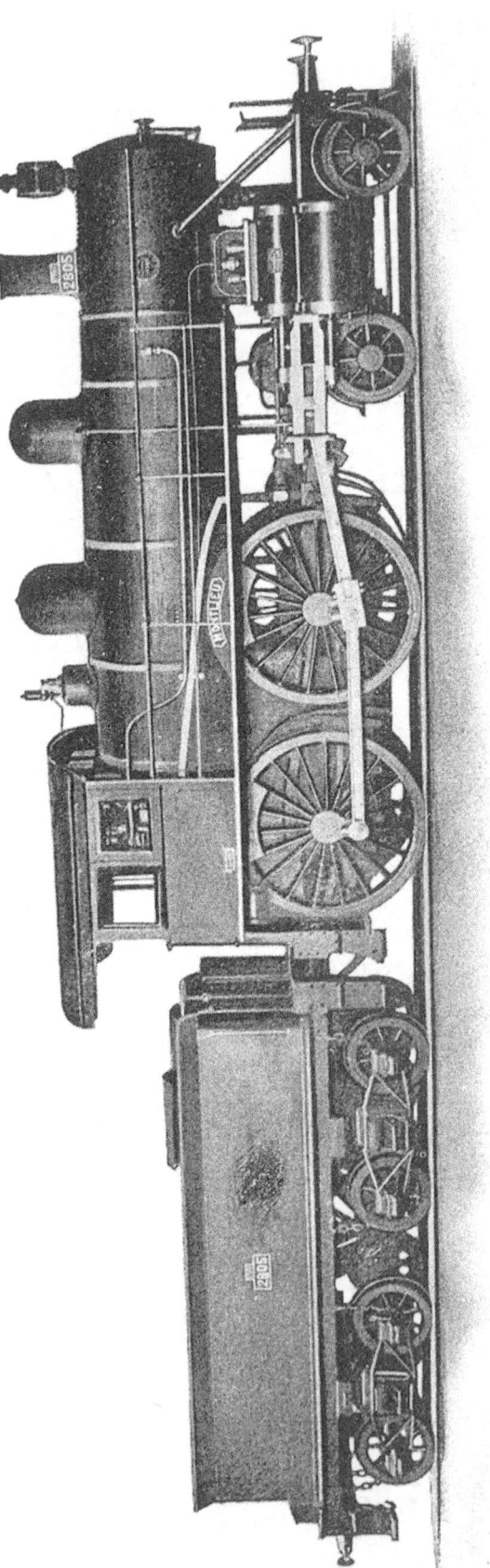

AMERICAN TYPE LOCOMOTIVE, FRENCH STATE RAILWAYS.

ENCLOSED SWITCHING LOCOMOTIVE.

Moscow-Keif-Voroneje	33
Moscow-Windau-Ribinsk	20
New Orleans and Northeastern	4
New York and New England	12
New York, Chicago and St. Louis	1
New York, Pennsylvania and Ohio	8
New Zealand Government Railways	8
Norfolk and Southern	3
Norfolk and Western	46
Northern Pacific	5

CONSOLIDATION LOCOMOTIVE, GRAND TRUNK RAILWAY.

CONSOLIDATION LOCOMOTIVE, PAULISTA RAILWAY OF BRAZIL.

VAUCLAIN COMPOUND. 63

Norwegian State Railways	4
Oeste de Minas, Brazil	22
Ottawa, Arnprior and Parry Sound	28
Oosoori Railway of Russia	1
Paulista Railway, Brazil	52
Pennsylvania	7
Pennsylvania and Northwestern	10
Pernambuco Extension, Brazil	7
Philadelphia and Reading	129
Philadelphia and Reading Coal and Iron Co.	4
Pikes Peak (rack)	5
Plymouth Cordage Co.	1
Ramal Dumont, Brazil	1
Ramal Ferreo Campineiro, Brazil	2

CONSOLIDATION LOCOMOTIVE, INTERCOLONIAL RAILWAY.

Rio Grande Western	4
Rockaway Valley	1
Rumford Falls and Rangeley Lakes	1
Salinas	1
Sandusky and Columbus Short Line	2
San José and Alum Rock, Hugh Centre	1
Santo Domingo (rack)	1
Sanyo Railway, Japan	7
Seaboard Air Line	2
S. Ellero and Vallombrosa (rack)	1

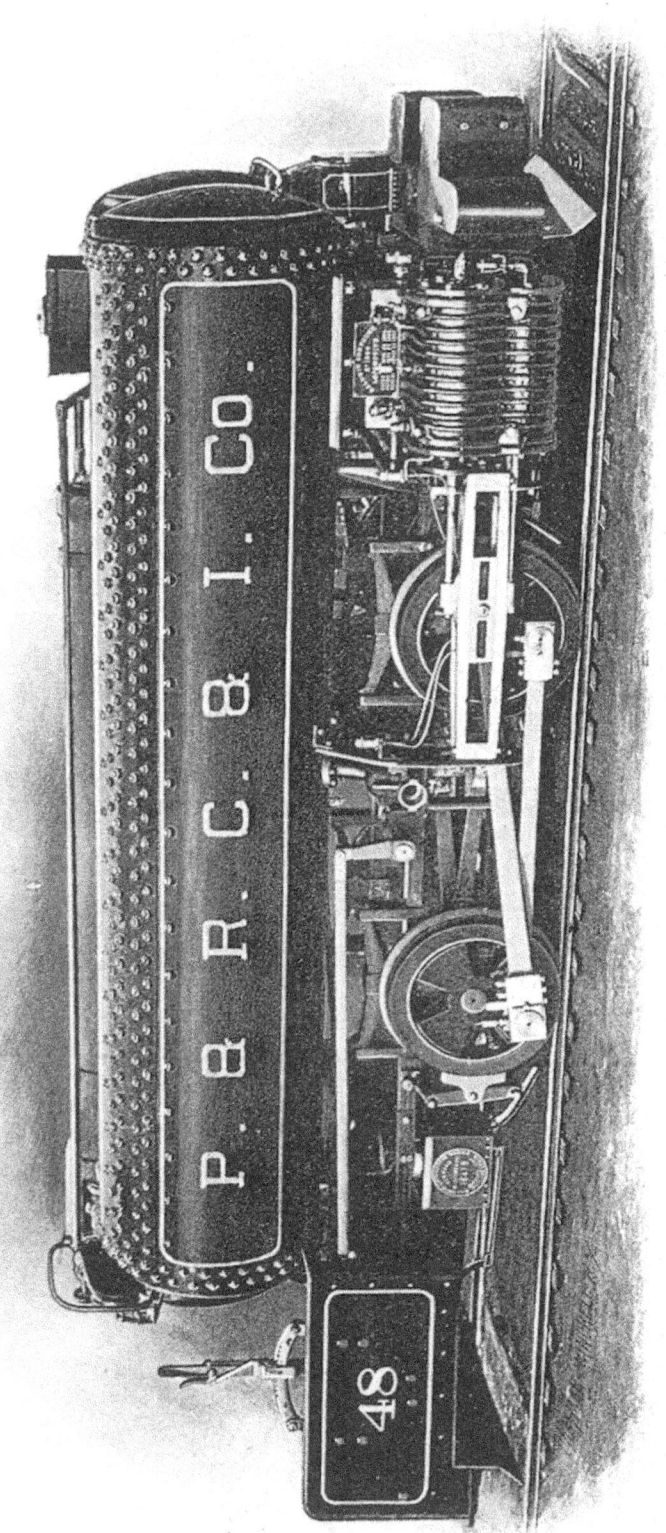
COMPRESSED AIR LOCOMOTIVE, PHILADELPHIA & READING COAL & IRON CO.

VAUCLAIN COMPOUND. 65

Sormovo Co., Ltd., Russia	3
Southeastern, Russia	69
Southern	1
State Transcaucasian, Russia	8
St. Louis and San Francisco	5
Texas and Pacific	1
Texas Central	4
Tikuho Railway of Japan	1
Toledo, Ann Arbor and North Michigan	6
Union Pacific	103
Union Terminal of Kansas City	1
United Verde Copper Co.	2
Virginia and Southwestern	6
Victorian Railways, Australia	2

AMERICAN TYPE LOCOMOTIVE, WABASH RAILROAD.

Vladicaucase of Russia	80
Wabash	3
Western Australia	20
Western Counties, Nova Scotia	2
Western Maryland	2
Western New York and Pennsylvania	1
Western Railway of Havana	1
West Virginia Central and Pittsburg	2
White Pass and Yukon	2
Wilmington Street Railway	1

TEN-WHEEL DOUBLE-ENDER PASSENGER LOCOMOTIVE, WELLINGTON & MANAWATU RAILWAY.

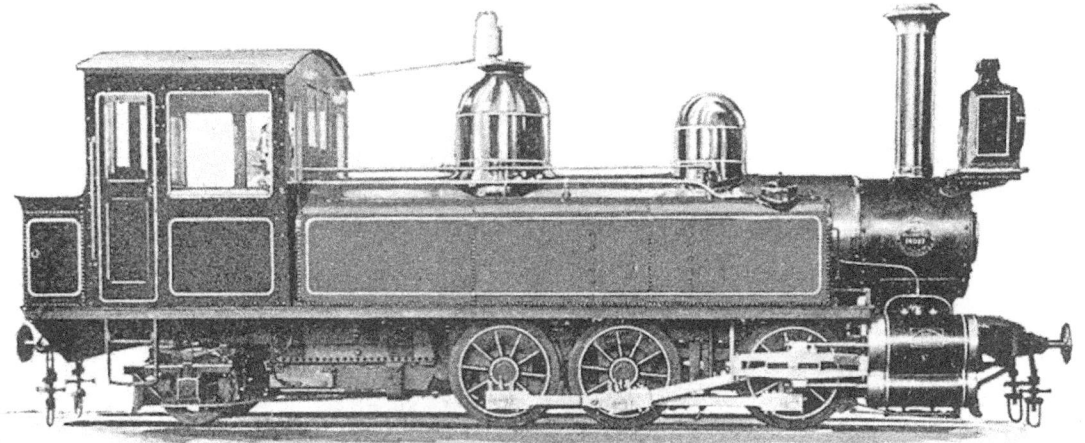

NARROW-GAUGE SIX-COUPLED TANK LOCOMOTIVE, STATE TRANSCAUCASIAN RAILWAY OF RUSSIA.

Comparative tests of Vauclain compound and single-expansion locomotives have been made by capable engineers, and usually under the supervision of the locomotive department of the respective lines.

Following is a summary of the general results:

In July, 1891, a test was made in freight service by Mr. John Hickey, Superintendent of Motive Power and Machinery of the Northern Pacific Railroad, the work being under the immediate supervision of Mr. O. H. Reynolds, then Mechanical Engineer for the company, of the compound Mogul locomotive No. 587, and a single expansion Mogul No. 584, both being of same

TEN-WHEEL PASSENGER LOCOMOTIVE, MISSOURI, KANSAS & TEXAS RAILWAY

NARROW-GAUGE CONSOLIDATION LOCOMOTIVE, WHITE PASS & YUKON RAILROAD.

dimensions and weight and differing only in the cylinders and boiler pressure.

Separate tests were made, (1) with both locomotives carrying 170 pounds of steam pressure, (2) with the compound carrying 170 and the single-expansion carrying 150 pounds pressure, and (3) with both locomotives carrying 150 pounds pressure. The average steam pressure carried for all trips by the compound locomotive was 157.3, and by the single-expansion locomotive was 151.9 pounds. The course was between Staples, Minnesota, and Fargo, Dakota, a distance of 108.7 miles. The trains were

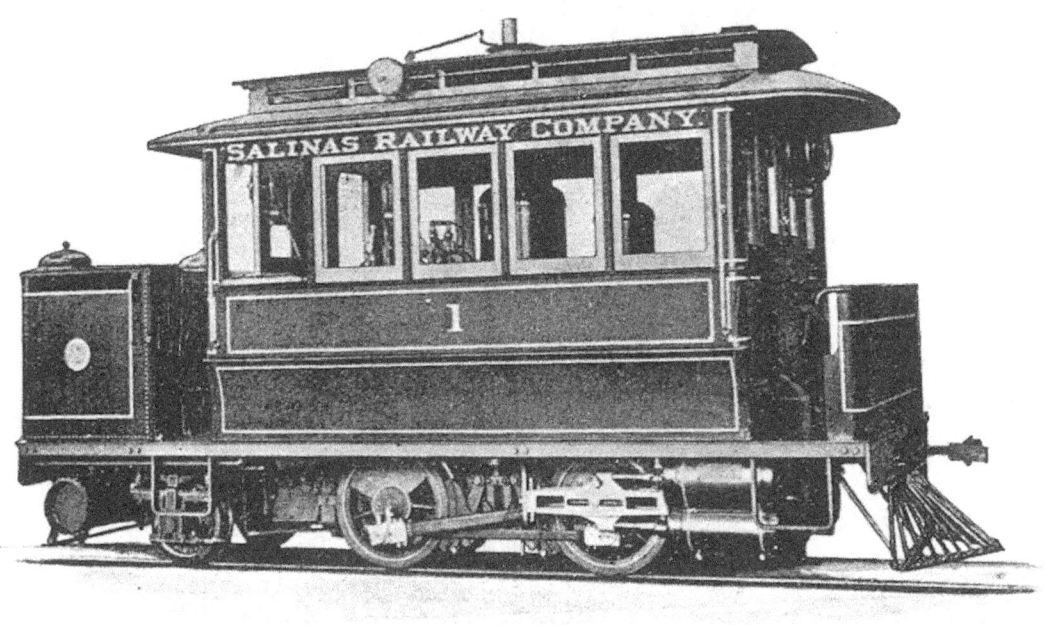

ENCLOSED MOTOR, SALINAS RAILWAY.

selected to give each locomotive as nearly the same weight as possible.

Five trips were run with both locomotives carrying 170 pounds of steam, the average result showing a saving in fuel of 28 per cent. in favor of the compound locomotive. On one trip where the compound locomotive was loaded to its most economical limit, a saving of 53.5 per cent. was made.

Four trips were run with the single-expansion locomotive carrying 150 pounds of steam and the compound carrying 170

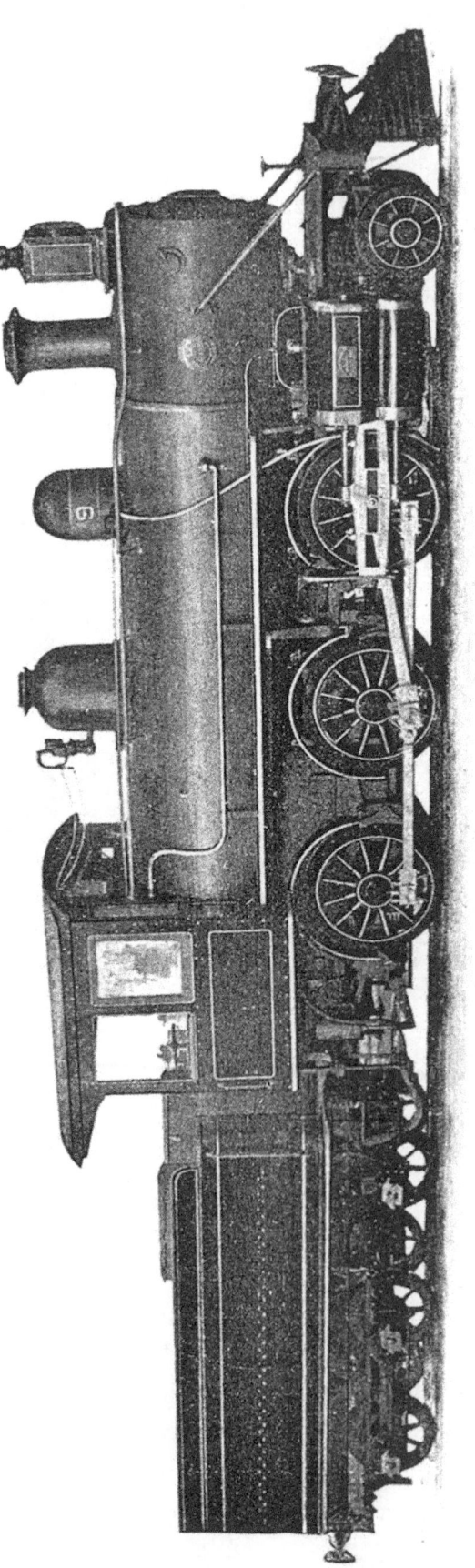

MOGUL LOCOMOTIVE, TIKU HO RAILWAY JAPAN.

pounds, the average result showing a saving of 20.9 per cent. in favor of the compound locomotive. One trip was run with both locomotives carrying 150 pounds of steam, which showed a saving of 18.3 per cent. in favor of the compound locomotive.

The general average of the ten trips gave a total saving in favor of the compound locomotive of 22.2 per cent. in fuel and 11.27 per cent. in water evaporated per pound of coal. The waste gases in the smoke-box of the single-expansion locomotive reached a temperature of 878 deg., while the highest registered by the compound was 590 deg. Fahrenheit.

CONSOLIDATION LOCOMOTIVE GOVERNMENT RAILWAYS OF VICTORIA.

The highest smoke-box vacuum in the single-expansion locomotive was 6 ounces or about 10 inches, and in the compound 4 ounces or about 6¾ inches.

In August and September, 1891, a test was made in freight service by Mr. Allen Vail, General Master Mechanic of the Western New York and Pennsylvania Railroad, of the compound consolidation locomotive No. 175, and single-expansion consolidation No. 169, both locomotives being identical except the cylinders.

The tests were made with the compound locomotive carrying 170 pounds steam pressure, and the single-expansion locomotive carrying 150 pounds. The average pressure carried for all trips by the compound was 166 pounds, and by the single-expansion 147.7 pounds. The course was between Buffalo and Olean, N. Y., a distance of 70 miles. Three round trips were run, with

TEN-WHEEL NARROW-GAUGE FREIGHT LOCOMOTIVE, OESTE DE MINAS, BRAZIL.

an average increase in favor of the compound locomotive of 36.2 per cent. in weight of train hauled per pound of coal, and of 17.9 per cent. in water evaporated per pound of coal.

The average temperature of the smoke-box gases was 690 deg. in the single-expansion locomotive, and 630 deg. in the compound.

The average smoke-box vacuum in the single-expansion locomotive was 6.4 inches, and in the compound 2.9 inches.

In January, 1892, a test was made in freight service by Mr. David Holtz, Master of Machinery of the Western Maryland Railroad, of compound consolidation locomotive No. 45, and a single-expansion consolidation locomotive No. 43, of similar size and dimensions with the exception of the cylinders.

The test was made on a mountain grade 10 miles in length with a total ascent of 1000 feet. At several points the grade reaches 105.6 feet per mile, with numerous sharp curves.

A single trip was made with each locomotive under similar conditions with the same train, the single-expansion locomotive carrying 147 pounds steam pressure, and the compound carrying 175 pounds.

The saving in fuel was 44.9 per cent. in favor of the compound locomotive. Quite a saving was also noted in the consumption of water.

In January, 1892, several tests were made, both in passenger and freight service, by Mr. R. H. Soule, Superintendent of Motive Power of the Norfolk and Western Railroad,—the work being under the supervision of Mr. George R. Henderson, Chief Draughtsman,—of the ten-wheel compound locomotive No. 82.

FRONT VIEW OF VAUCLAIN COMPOUND LOCOMOTIVE.

The test was made and the data of the performance noted for comparison with tests which had previously been made with similar single-expansion locomotives in the same service.

The average steam pressure carried by the compound locomotive was 181 pounds, and that carried by the single-expansion locomotives with which it was compared was 139 pounds. The course over which the run was made in passenger service was between Roanoke and Bristol, a distance of 150 miles, and that for freight service between West Roanoke and Radford, a distance of 41.6 miles. Four round trips were made with a passenger train and two round trips with freight. Comparing the general average with that of the single-expansion locomotives, it was found that the compound showed a saving in fuel of nearly 38 per cent. per ton per mile, with a corresponding saving in water.

Average smoke-box vacuum was in the compound 2¼ inches, and in the single-expansion 5 inches.

In 1892 a test was made on the Chicago, Milwaukee and St. Paul Railroad, by a committee appointed by the Master Mechanics' Association of compound locomotive No. 827, and the single-expansion locomotive No. 822, of precisely the same construction excepting the cylinders. The tests extended over a period of nearly two months, sixty complete single trips being made, the locomotives carrying 180 and 200 pounds pressure of steam. The route selected was from Milwaukee to Portage, a distance of 91 miles.

AMERICAN TYPE LOCOMOTIVE PAULISTA RAILWAY, BRAZIL.

ATLANTIC TYPE LOCOMOTIVE, PHILADELPHIA & READING RAILROAD.

The average economy of the compound locomotive was placed at 16.9 per cent. in fuel and 14.1 per cent. in water.

In September and October, 1892, a test was made in passenger service by Mr. James Meehan, Superintendent of Motive Power and Machinery of the Cincinnati, New Orleans and Texas Pacific Railway, of the ten-wheel compound locomotive No. 604, and a single expansion locomotive of the same type, No. 531.

The tests were made with both limited and accommodation trains, the compound locomotive carrying 180 pounds pressure of steam, and the single expansion 140 pounds. The average

NARROW-GAUGE LOCOMOTIVE NORWEGIAN STATE RAILWAY.

steam pressure shown by the indicator cards was for the compound 173.3 pounds, and for the single-expansion 133.3 pounds. The distance run was 93.3 miles. Ten trips were made with each locomotive. The average results showed a total saving in consumption of fuel in favor of the compound locomotive of 35½ per cent. in pounds of coal per car mile, but as the compound locomotive had a somewhat larger amount of heating surface, it was thought best to place the gain at 25 per cent., in order to be sure and on the safe side.

In November, 1893, a series of tests was made in freight

MOGUL LOCOMOTIVE, MISSOURI, KANSAS & TEXAS RAILWAY.

service by Mr. Chas. M. Jacobs, Consulting Engineer of the Long Island Railroad, and his assistant, Mr. J. V. Davies, of the ten-wheel freight locomotive No. 145 and the ten-wheel single-expansion locomotive No. 138. It was arranged in this test to run three consecutive trips with each locomotive with a train of twenty loaded cars set apart for the purpose, in order that each locomotive should do the same work under the same conditions. The steam pressure carried by the compound locomotive was 180 pounds and by the single-expansion locomotive 145 pounds.

The average steam pressure was, for the compound, 166.7 pounds, and for the single-expansion 126 pounds.

The course was between Hempstead Crossing and Ronkonkoma, and the train was hauled the round trip twice, making a distance of 113.78 miles.

The general average of these trips showed an economy in fuel of 37.2 per cent., and in water of 10.7 per cent., per car mile, in favor of the compound locomotive.

In December, 1893, and January, 1894, a series of tests was made in passenger service by Mr. L. B. Paxson, Superintendent of Motive Power and Rolling Equipment of the Philadelphia and Reading Railroad, of the compound "Columbia" type locomotive No. 694, and the single-expansion American type locomotive No. 1016.

These tests were conducted (1) to determine the difference of economy of the two locomotives and (2) to ascertain if it were possible to use buckwheat or pea coal in high-speed passenger service. Separate tests were made with the locomotives burning egg, pea, and buckwheat coal.

The average steam pressure for the compound was 169.6 pounds, and for the single-expansion 152.9 pounds.

The course was between Camden and Atlantic City, a distance of 55.5 miles.

The results showed that when both locomotives burned egg coal, a saving was made in favor of the compound of 26.9 per cent. When both locomotives burned pea coal the saving in favor of the compound was 27.3 per cent., and a comparison between the single-expansion locomotive burning egg coal and

MOGUL LOCOMOTIVE BRAZILIAN INDUSTRIAL IMPROVEMENT CO.

VAUCLAIN COMPOUND.

CONSOLIDATION LOCOMOTIVE, BALTIMORE & OHIO RAILROAD.

TEN-WHEEL PASSENGER LOCOMOTIVE, ALTOONA, CLEARFIELD & NORTHERN RAILROAD.

the compound burning pea coal still showed a saving of 6.9 per cent. in actual weight; but when the difference of cost is considered the saving would be 68.6 per cent. in favor of the compound. It was demonstrated by these tests that pea coal could be satisfactorily used on high-speed passenger service in compound locomotives only, and also that the compound locomotive would do better with pea coal as fuel than the single-expansion locomotive with egg coal.

In August, 1894, a test was made in freight and passenger service by Mr. J. E. Fulton, Locomotive Superintendent of the Wellington and Manawatu Railway (a narrow-gauge road in New Zealand), of the ten-wheeled compound passenger locomotive No. 14, shown by the illustration on page 66, and the compound consolidation freight locomotive No. 13, the latter in competition with the single-expansion consolidation locomotive No. 12, of similar weight and dimensions.

The crucial test was on a section of the road where a grade of 1 to 100 occurred. This grade was three miles in length, and the compound ran it easily with 83 cars or 350 tons, exclusive of its own weight of 56 tons, at a rate of 6 miles an hour; the usual load for the company's best locomotives of the single expansion type on this grade being 45 cars or 250 tons.

The result of the test showed a saving in fuel with the compound locomotive of exactly 25 per cent., and the trip was made in quicker time than with the single-expansion.

VAUCLAIN COMPOUND.

AMERICAN TYPE LOCOMOTIVE, CHILEAN STATE RAILWAY.

In April, 1894, a series of tests was made on the Central Railroad of New Jersey, in passenger service, of the compound locomotive No. 450 of the American type, and the single-expansion passenger locomotive No. 455, of similar dimensions.

These tests were conducted by Mr. Russell E. Taylor, M. E., Mr. Chas. C. Kenyon, M. E., and Mr. Edward D. Mathey, M. E., a committee from Stevens Institute of Technology, the object being to ascertain comparatively (1) the evaporation from and at 212 deg. Fahrenheit per pound of coal, (2) the water per hour per horse-power, (3) the coal used per ton of total train mile, and (4) the action of the engines under various conditions.

PLANTATION LOCOMOTIVE, RAMAL DUMONT, BRAZIL.

The course was between Jersey City and Wayne Junction, a distance of 85.1 miles.

Two round trips were made with each locomotive. The average boiler pressure carried was for the compound 164.9 pounds, and for the single-expansion 157.5 pounds.

The general results obtained show a percentage in favor of the compound locomotive as follows:

In coal consumed during test . . . . 19.86 per cent.
In water evaporated from and at 212° per pound
    of coal on run . . . . 18.7 per cent.
In rate of combustion per sq. ft. of grate per hour
    during run . . . . 20.05 per cent.
In tons of train hauled per mile per pound of
    coal . . . . 15.85 per cent.

VAUCLAIN COMPOUND.

83

AMERICAN TYPE LOCOMOTIVE, ERIE RAILROAD.

TEN-WHEEL FREIGHT LOCOMOTIVE, CENTRAL RAILROAD OF NEW JERSEY

The record of one ten-wheel compound and nine single-expansion locomotives of the same type, differing only in the construction of the cylinders, taken from the monthly performance sheets issued by Mr. John Mackenzie, Superintendent of Motive Power of the New York, Chicago and St. Louis Railroad, for nine months, from November, 1892, to July, 1893, gives an average consumption of fuel per mile run for the compound locomotive of 3.1 pounds, and for the single-expansion locomotive 4 pounds, making a total saving in favor of the compound locomotive of 22.5 per cent.

In October, 1896, a test was made in freight service, under the direction of Mr. John Hickey, Superintendent M. P. & R. S. of the Northern Pacific Railroad, and under the immediate supervision of Mr. W. B. Norton, Road Foreman of Engines, of a compound consolidation locomotive, No. 488, and a single-expansion consolidation locomotive, No. 492.

As originally built these locomotives were of the same size and general design, the single-expansion cylinders of No. 488 having been subsequently replaced by compound cylinders.

The test was made on the portion of the Northern Pacific Line between Leslie and the summit of the Cascade Mountains, a distance of 16.1 miles, on an average grade of 116 feet per mile.

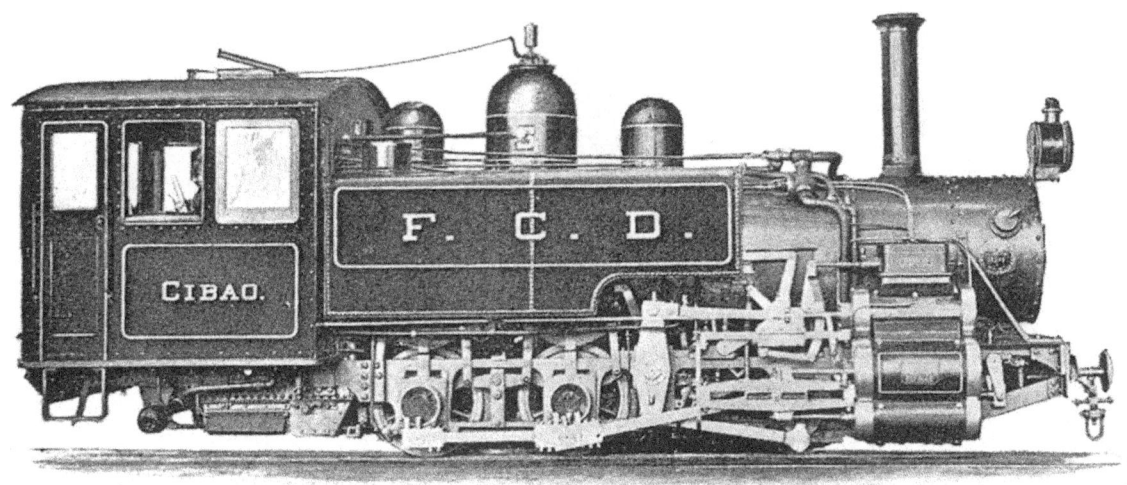

RACK AND ADHESION LOCOMOTIVE, SANTO DOMINGO RAILWAY.

Out of a number of trips run, three were selected as having all the conditions comparatively equal. These show an average consumption of coal by the compound locomotive of 2976 lbs., and by the single-expansion locomotive of 5521 lbs. The average water evaporation by the compound was 2622 gallons, and by the single-expansion 3759 gallons. The average load was 435 tons hauled by the compound and 430 tons hauled by the single-expansion.

The results show a saving in favor of the compound locomotive of forty-six per cent. in the consumption of fuel, and thirty per cent. in the evaporation.

The following table gives the actual running time for one trip made by locomotive No. 1028, with a train of five cars, July 1, 1898, on the Atlantic City Division of the Philadelphia and Reading Railway.

The locomotive is illustrated by the cut of No. 1027, on page 76, which is of same type and dimensions. It will be noted that a single mile was made in 41 seconds, which indicates a speed of 87.8 miles per hour. An average speed of 81.8 miles

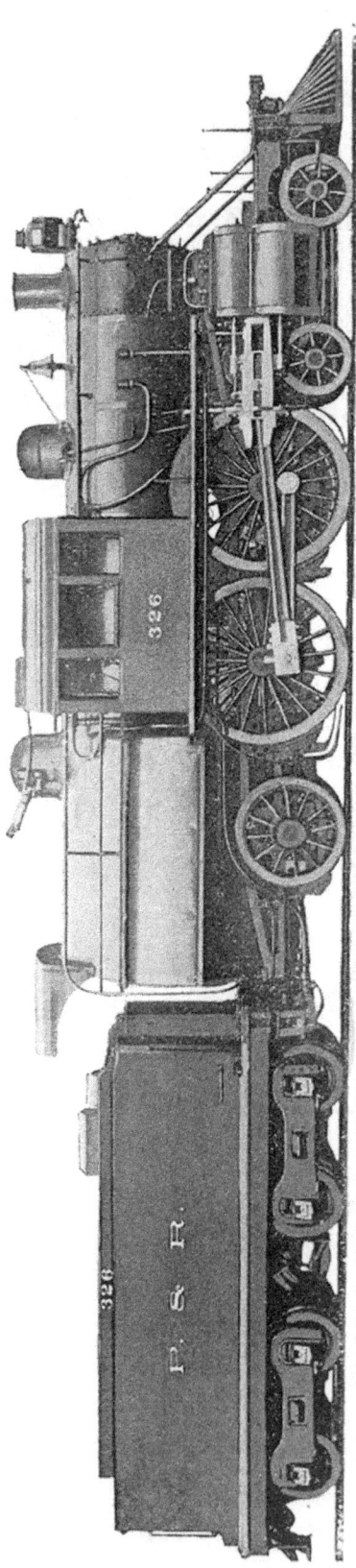

ATLANTIC TYPE LOCOMOTIVE, PHILADELPHIA & READING RAILWAY.

per hour was maintained between mile-posts 48 and 3, a distance of 45 miles. This includes some of the heaviest grades on the division. For 36 miles, or from mile-post 39 to mile-post 3, the distance was covered at an average speed of 82.8 miles per hour.

Mile-Posts.	Time. H.	M.	S.	Seconds per Mile.	Mile-Posts.	Time. H.	M.	S.	Seconds per Mile.
Camden	3	50	00	00	27	4	14	55	42
55	3	52	29	149	26	4	15	37	42
54	3	53	44	75	25	4	16	20	43
53	3	54	43	59	24	4	17	03	43
52	3	55	39	56	23	4	17	46	43
51	3	56	34	55	22	4	18	30	44
50	3	57	28	54	21	4	19	15	45
49	3	58	18	50	20	4	19	59	44
48	3	59	08	50	19	4	20	43	44
47	3	59	55	47	18	4	21	25	42
46	4	00	42	47	17	4	22	08	43
45	4	01	28	46	16	4	22	51	43
44	4	02	11	43	15	4	23	34	43
43	4	02	56	45	14	4	24	18	44
42	4	03	43	47	13	4	25	03	45
41	4	04	32	49	12	4	25	48	45
40	4	05	21	49	11	4	26	32	44
39	4	06	10	49	10	4	27	15	43
38	4	06	56	46	9	4	27	59	44
37	4	07	41	45	8	4	28	42	43
36	4	08	24	43	7	4	29	25	43
35	4	09	08	44	6	4	30	09	44
34	4	09	52	44	5	4	30	51	42
33	4	10	37	45	4	4	31	32	41
32	4	11	20	43	3	4	32	16	44
31	4	12	03	43	2	4	33	07	51
30	4	12	47	44	1	4	34	15	68
29	4	13	30	43	Atlantic City	4	35	17	62 ½ mile
28	4	14	13	43					

Time, 45 minutes 17 seconds.

TRAIN NO. 25, ON THE ATLANTIC CITY RAILROAD, UNDER SPEED.

VAUCLAIN COMPOUND. 89

PERFORMANCE OF TRAIN No. 25. ON THE ATLANTIC CITY RAILROAD (PHILADELPHIA & READING ROUTE) FOR THE MONTHS OF JULY AND AUGUST, 1898.

Copy of Train Despatcher's sheet, showing exact running time of train, to which is added a statement showing number of cars in train, number of passengers carried, and average number of miles per hour for each trip.

[Table of train performance data for July and August 1898, showing for each day of the month at each station (Camden, West Collingswood, Haddon Heights, Magnolia, Clementon, Williamstown Junction, Cedar Brook, Winslow Junction, Hammonton, Elwood, Egg Harbor, Brigantine Junction, Pleasantville, Meadow Tower, Atlantic City) with distance column and scheduled time column, followed by daily columns with running times; plus summary rows for Number of cars, Passengers carried, Running time, and Miles per hour (average).]

ATLANTIC TYPE LOCOMOTIVE, CHICAGO, MILWAUKEE & ST. PAUL RAILROAD

VAUCLAIN COMPOUND.

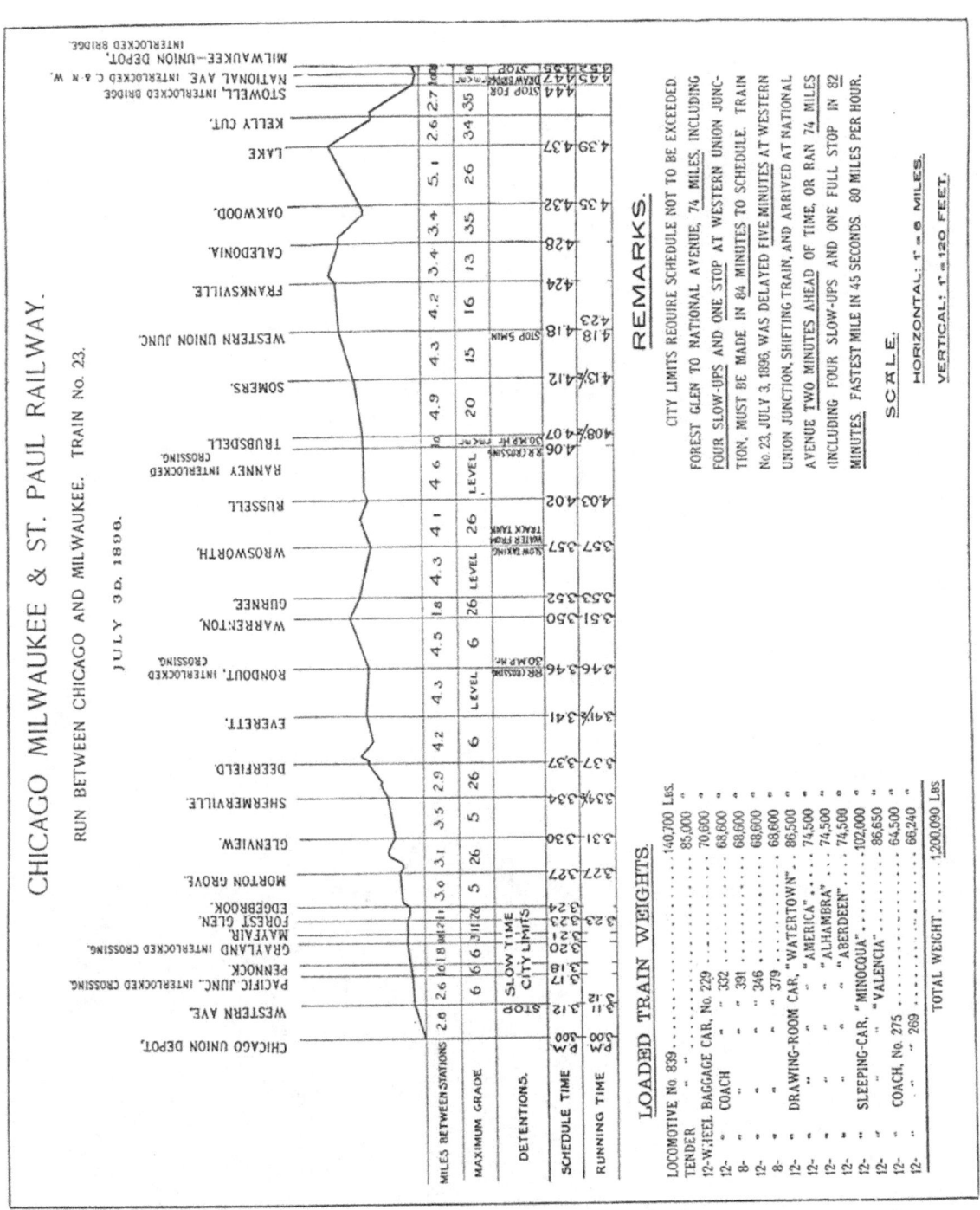

Complete detailed reports of the foregoing tests, with indicator diagrams, are on file in the office of the Baldwin Locomotive Works, and can be examined by any one interested.

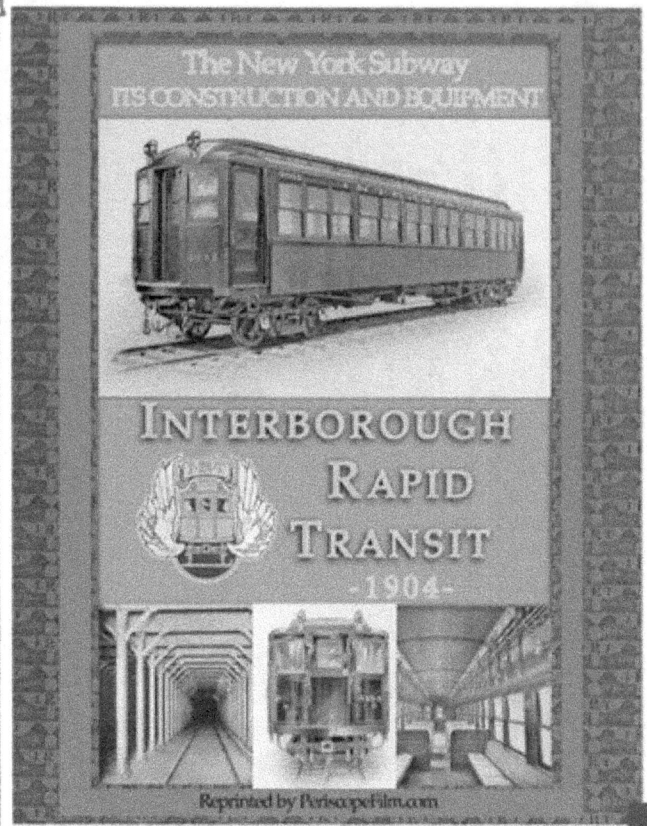

On October 27, 1904, the Interborough Rapid Transit Company opened the first subway in New York City. Running between City Hall and 145th Street at Broadway, the line was greeted with enthusiasm and, in some circles, trepidation. Created under the supervision of Chief Engineer S.L.F. Deyo, the arrival of the IRT foreshadowed the end of the "elevated" transit era on the island of Manhattan. The subway proved such a success that the IRT Co. soon achieved a monopoly on New York public transit. In 1940 the IRT and its rival the BMT were taken over by the City of New York. Today, the IRT subway lines still exist, primarily in Manhattan where they are operated as the "A Division" of the subway. Reprinted here is a special book created by the IRT, recounting the design and construction of the fledgling subway system. Originally created in 1904, it presents the IRT story with a flourish, and with numerous fascinating illustrations and rare photographs.

Originally written in the late 1900's and then periodically revised, A History of the Baldwin Locomotive Works chronicles the origins and growth of one of America's greatest industrial-era corporations. Founded in the early 1830's by Philadelphia jeweler Matthais Baldwin, the company built a huge number of steam locomotives before ceasing production in 1949. These included the 4-4-0 American type, 2-8-2 Mikado and 2-8-0 Consolidation. Hit hard by the loss of the steam engine market, Baldwin soldiered on for a brief while, producing electric and diesel engines. General Electric's dominance of the market proved too much, and Baldwin finally closed its doors in 1956. By that time over 70,500 Baldwin locomotives had been produced. This high quality reprint of the official company history dates from 1920. The book has been slightly reformatted, but care has been taken to preserve the integrity of the text.

NOW AVAILABLE AT
WWW.PERISCOPEFILM.COM

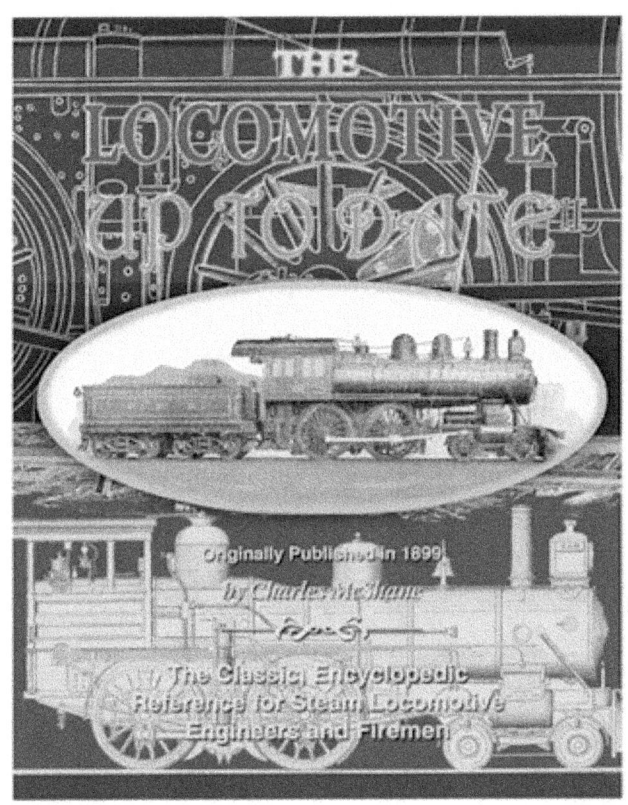

When it was originally published in 1899, **The Locomotive Up to Date** was hailed as "...the most definitive work ever published concerning the mechanism that has transformed the American nation: the steam locomotive." Filled with over 700 pages of text, diagrams and photos, this remains one of the most important railroading books ever written. From steam valves to sanders, trucks to side rods, it's a treasure trove of information, explaining in easy-to-understand language how the most sophisticated machines of the 19th Century were operated and maintained. This new edition is an exact duplicate of the original. Reformatted as an easy-to-read 8.5x11 volume, it's delightful for railroad enthusiasts of all ages.

Originally printed in 1898 and then periodically revised, **The Motorman...and His Duties** served as the definitive training text for a generation of streetcar operators. A must-have for the trolley or train enthusiast, it is also an important source of information for museum staff and docents. Lavishly illustrated with numerous photos and black and white line drawings, this affordable reprint contains all of the original text. Includes chapters on trolley car types and equipment, troubleshooting, brakes, controllers, electricity and principles, electric traction, multi-car control and has a convenient glossary in the back. If you've ever operated a trolley car, or just had an electric train set, this is a terrific book for your shelf!

ALSO NOW AVAILABLE FROM PERISCOPEFILM.COM!

©2007-2010 Periscope Film LLC
All Rights Reserved
ISBN #978-1-935700-15-9
www.PeriscopeFilm.com

www.ingramcontent.com/pod-product-compliance
Lightning Source LLC
LaVergne TN
LVHW061346060426
835512LV00012B/2580